ONE-
MINUTE
MEMORY
BOOSTERS

Other Books by Frank Minirth

Happiness Is a Choice
Introduction to Psychology and Counseling
A Brilliant Mind
Choosing Happiness When Life Is Hard
Boost Your Brainpower
You Can!

ONE-MINUTE MEMORY BOOSTERS

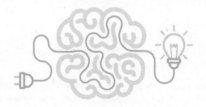

FRANK MINIRTH, MD

SPIRE

© 2017 by Minirth Holdings, LLC

Published by Revell
a division of Baker Publishing Group
PO Box 6287, Grand Rapids, MI 49516-6287
www.revellbooks.com

This Spire edition published 2022
ISBN 978-0-8007-4145-7 (paperback)
ISBN 978-1-4934-3634-7 (ebook)

Material adapted from *Memory Builders*, published by Spire in 2021, originally published under the title *Strong Memory, Sharp Mind* by Revell in 2017.

Printed in the United States of America

The names and details of the people and situations described in this book have been changed or presented in composite form in order to ensure the privacy of those with whom the author has worked.

This publication is intended to provide helpful and informative material on the subjects addressed. Readers should consult their personal health professionals before adopting any of the suggestions in this book or drawing inferences from it. The author and publisher expressly disclaim responsibility for any adverse effects arising from the use or application of the information contained in this book.

Baker Publishing Group publications use paper produced from sustainable forestry practices and post-consumer waste whenever possible.

22   23   24   25   26   27   28   7   6   5   4   3   2   1

Contents

Introduction   9

PART 1 **Assessment**   13

PART 2 **Memory Boosters**   21

PART 3 **Stress and Your Brain**   127

PART 4 **Anxiety and Your Brain**   143

PART 5 **Memory and Purpose**   155

Conclusion   177
Appendix: Answer Key   179
Bibliography   183
Notes   187

Brain on Board

You don't see it or feel it. You can't hear it or hold it.

It's out of sight, out of mind.

Don't drift through your thirties, forties, and fifties,

then suddenly realize your brain is fading.

Don't settle for it being just "good enough."

You deserve better than that.

Don't take your brain for granted.

Introduction

Memory Matters

At birthday celebrations, I hear phrases such as "the thirties are the new twenties," "the forties are the new thirties," and "the fifties are the new forties." People brag about looking and feeling younger than their parents did at the same chronological age.

We want our minds to stay dynamic too. But after high school or college, some people never pick up another book or take another class. The more fit we keep our brains, the better they'll withstand the rigors of aging, protect our well-being, and lead to life satisfaction.

Everyone wants to be happy, healthy, loved, and reasonably prosperous and to enjoy fulfilling relationships. These core desires keep us motivated. Our decisions are based on these desires as well as habits, others' demands, impulsive urges, and conscious planning. And every day we choose what thoughts to dwell on and words to say, and what to do and not do. Each choice has far-reaching ramifications. Bit by bit, we form patterns that direct our lives and interpersonal interactions.

Something you may not have considered is that none of this is possible without a healthy brain. Your mind controls behavior, and if your mental status is compromised, days, weeks, months, and years can be difficult for you and your family.

I hope this book will motivate you to refresh healthy choices. It's okay to start with the easiest steps. Just start.

Don't Just Let Nature Take Its Course

If you've hit your early thirties, your brain's natural aging process has started. It may take longer to memorize and learn new things, and your verbal fluency, perception, and reasoning skills are slowing down.

Changes in the mind and body continue through every life phase. But the older we get, the more dramatic the symptoms seem: our hair and skin look different, and memories often begin to fade. This impacts everyone at some point, but there is help and hope to keep our minds intact through the senior years.

Do You Want a Sharper Mind? It's Possible at Any Age

When one of my daughters was young, I asked, "Do you want to boost your brainpower?" She did. Today, she is a medical doctor and psychiatrist.

In response to a frail, elderly pastor's request for help with his fading memory, I asked, "Do you want to boost your brainpower?" He did. He has returned to preaching and is enjoying a thriving ministry.

It's encouraging to know that brainpower can be increased at any age—through childhood, adolescence, young adulthood, adulthood, and even in the senior years. The benefits of controlling, challenging, directing, and improving our minds are many, including delaying cognitive decline or slowing the progression of Alzheimer's disease.

A Personal Note

When I graduated from medical school, I took the Hippocratic Oath, which is traditional for physicians as they begin medical practice. Several phrases from that pledge have inspired me throughout my career to promote preventive mental health care to help people avoid or lessen the devastating effects of mental illness.

Here are some excerpts:

> I will prevent disease whenever I can for prevention is preferable to cure.

> I will remember that I remain a member of society, with special obligations to all my fellow human beings, those sound of mind and body as well as the infirm.

The books I've written and the years of hosting radio talk shows were in response to these commitments. I have focused on educating people about mental health so they can be aware of and recognize problems in the early stages. This book is my continued "call to action" to encourage everyone to protect their mind and their long-term quality of life.

Dr. Frank Minirth

PART 1

ASSESSMENT

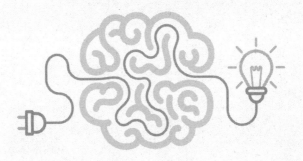

It's Your Choice

Your choices chart your life, for better or worse. If you're in your thirties or forties, you've got the time, momentum, and some life experience going for you. To be healthy, your brain needs regular exercise, rest, nutrition, and tune-ups. Daily choices can be just as important as the major decisions you make. Are your lifestyle choices hurting or helping your brain health?

Take this quick quiz.

	Yes	No
Do you eat junk food and sugar?	___	___
Do you sit the majority of the day?	___	___
Do you spend hours watching television or surfing the internet?	___	___
Do you generally feel stressed or anxious?	___	___
Do you spend more time watching television than reading books or exercising?	___	___
Do you spend most of your days alone?	___	___
Do you have a chronic illness?	___	___
Do you have an unhealthy addiction?	___	___
Do you have a weight problem?	___	___
Do you get less than seven hours of sleep at night?	___	___

The more yes answers you have, the more you may need a brain-care tune-up.

Why Do You Want a Sharper Mind?

Place a check mark by all the following motives that apply to you. This will encourage you to step up your brain fitness. It may also help you clarify your short- and long-range goals, strengths, and areas for improvement.

I want to build my brainpower so I can

- [ ] decrease the chance of memory loss in later years
- [ ] maintain my current level of memory and brain function
- [ ] improve my self-esteem
- [ ] maintain independence as long as possible
- [ ] improve my decision-making and problem-solving skills
- [ ] facilitate my career advancement
- [ ] improve my short- and long-term memory
- [ ] avoid embarrassing situations (i.e., brain freeze, senior moments)
- [ ] improve my attention span and concentration
- [ ] improve my scholastic performance
- [ ] do more multitasking (which is really changing sharp focus very quickly)

- [ ] be more efficient in daily routines
- [ ] consistently function at my best level
- [ ] improve my relationships
- [ ] function better in business and social situations (i.e., remember names and details)
- [ ] reduce the stress of managing all my responsibilities
- [ ] accentuate my personal strengths
- [ ] have more intelligent conversations
- [ ] enjoy more special interests and activities
- [ ] stop or reverse cognitive decline (cognition is the mental process of acquiring knowledge and understanding through thought, experience, and the senses)

Self-Assessment:
How Am I Doing?

There's a lot to be said for motivation, common sense, and mental fitness. They serve you well in everything you do.

As much as possible, choose to stay in a healthy zone—mentally, physically, emotionally, and spiritually. Being in constant pursuit of self-improvement is a process that requires a series of good choices. There is truth in the adage "We make our choices, then our choices make us."

When evaluating your personal brain health, the following factors can guide you. This is a snapshot of current stressors that may be impeding your mental and physical health.

Note: This brief self-assessment may be influenced by your current state of mind, depending on whether you are feeling confident or stressed out. Consider each of the following issues from an honest, general, insightful viewpoint.

Place a check mark by each of the areas that you may need help with or that may need some improvement in your life:

☐ general functioning   ☐ mood

☐ illness   ☐ healthy choices

☐ relationships   ☐ exercise

☐ addictions   ☐ learning new things

☐ medications/drugs   ☐ memory/cognition

- [ ] business arrangements
- [ ] anxiety
- [ ] pain level
- [ ] hobbies
- [ ] major, recent events/ changes
- [ ] family history
- [ ] abuse
- [ ] wasting time
- [ ] attitude
- [ ] physical symptoms
- [ ] diet
- [ ] job performance
- [ ] energy level
- [ ] productivity
- [ ] weight

- [ ] sensitivity
- [ ] decision-making
- [ ] stress level
- [ ] time management
- [ ] financial security
- [ ] confusion
- [ ] sleep habits
- [ ] appearance/grooming
- [ ] codependency (addiction to people, behaviors, or things)
- [ ] personality traits
- [ ] technology/TV habits
- [ ] self-esteem
- [ ] other issues

Self-Assessment: Are You a Lifelong Learner?

Lifelong learning is deliberate and voluntary. It's having a positive attitude toward personal and career opportunities. It can boost your confidence and self-esteem, make you less risk averse and more adaptable to change, help you enjoy a more satisfying personal life, and be fun.

Do you . . .

	Yes	No
believe you can keep your mind sharp?		
experience any mental decline?		
use your spare time wisely?		
know your natural learning style?		
use any memory techniques?		
want to improve your reading skills?		
have interest in improving your vocabulary?		
have the willpower to exercise your brain?		
have a clear life purpose?		
need to make any lifestyle changes?		
take advantage of workplace training?		
have any learning projects underway?		

PART 2

MEMORY BOOSTERS

What Do You Know?

Test your knowledge as well as rekindle old memory tracks with the following one hundred general knowledge facts. If you don't know the answers, please research the information online instead of just guessing. The information will last longer in your memory when you look up answers on your own. Once you've determined and recorded all the correct answers, review them often for several months to commit the knowledge to your long-term memory.

	True	False
1. Robert Frost, the most popular twentieth-century American poet, wrote "The Road Not Taken" and "Stopping by Woods on a Snowy Evening."	____	____
2. Are the following definitions correct?		
a. biology—the study of living things	____	____
c. chemistry—the study of elements, compounds, and their reactions	____	____
b. physics—the study of the interaction of matter and energy	____	____
d. English—the study of the parts of speech	____	____
e. geology—the study of the earth	____	____
3. Hydrogen has an atomic number of 1.	____	____

	True	False
4. A laser is a beam of light.	___	___
5. Are the following associations correct?	___	___

United States of America	Washington, DC
Mexico	Mexico City
Russia	Moscow
Switzerland	Bern
United Kingdom	London
Spain	Madrid
Iran	Tehran
Iraq	Baghdad
Japan	Tokyo
Australia	Canberra
Egypt	Cairo
Bahamas	Nassau

	True	False
6. Currencies vary with the country. Are the following associations correct?	___	___

USA	dollar
Russia	ruble
Switzerland	franc
Mexico	peso
Saudi Arabia	riyal
United Kingdom	pound
Israel	shekel
South Africa	rand
Ghana (Gold Coast)	cedi
Iraq	dinar
China	yuan
Japan	yen
Sweden	krona

	True	False
7. The Alps are in Switzerland, and the Himalayas are in Nepal.	___	___

	True	False
8. The abbreviation for "for example" is e.g., and the abbreviation for "namely" is viz.	___	___
9. AM is amplitude modulation in radio signals; FM is frequency modulation.	___	___
10. Sandra Day O'Connor was the first female Supreme Court justice; Sally Ride was America's first female astronaut.	___	___
11. The largest countries by land size in order are:	___	___

  1. Russia
  2. Canada
  3. United States of America
  4. China
  5. Brazil
  6. Australia
  7. India
  8. Argentina
  9. Kazakhstan
  10. Algeria

12. The largest continents in order are: ___ ___

  1. Asia
  2. Africa
  3. North America
  4. South America
  5. Europe
  6. Antarctica
  7. Australia

13. The largest oceans in order are: ___ ___

  1. Pacific
  2. Atlantic
  3. Indian
  4. Antarctic
  5. Arctic

	True	False
14. Farming villages around the Mediterranean Gulf appeared around 10,000 BC.	____	____
15. Geometry started around 1000 BC.	____	____
16. The Olympic Games started in 776 BC.	____	____
17. Leif Erikson reached North America around 1000 AD.	____	____
18. Marco Polo traveled to China in 1271.	____	____
19. Bartolomeu Dias sailed around the southern tip of Africa (the Cape of Good Hope) in 1488.	____	____
20. Christopher Columbus discovered America in 1492.	____	____
21. Vasco Núñez de Balboa saw the Pacific Ocean in 1513.	____	____
22. Ferdinand Magellan sailed around the world in 1519–22.	____	____
23. The Great Lakes are: H—Huron O—Ontario M—Michigan E—Erie S—Superior	____	____
24. The average person in the United States watches television more than five hours per day.	____	____
25. Madison Avenue's business and economics district made New York City popular.	____	____

	True	False
26. The sculptures of four US presidents on Mount Rushmore include Washington, Jefferson, Lincoln, and Theodore Roosevelt.	___	___
27. The first permanent English settlement in North America was Jamestown, Virginia, in 1607.	___	___
28. The US military academy, West Point, is located in New York State.	___	___
29. The smallest continent is Australia.	___	___
30. The Black Sea is located between two continents, Europe and Asia.	___	___
31. The countries of Central America are Belize, Costa Rica, El Salvador, Guatemala, Honduras, Nicaragua, and Panama.	___	___
32. The country with the largest population is China.	___	___
33. The lowest point on earth is the Dead Sea at approximately 1,385 feet below sea level.	___	___
34. The capital of Scotland is Edinburgh.	___	___
35. Greenland is part of Denmark.	___	___
36. The former name of Iran is Persia.	___	___
37. Latitude refers to the north and south directions off the equator.	___	___
38. One of the smallest countries in the world is Liechtenstein (62 square miles) in the Alps between Austria and Switzerland.	___	___
39. The highest mountain in the world is Mount Everest.	___	___

	True	False
40. There are seven continents on planet Earth surrounded by five oceans.		
41. The largest and deepest ocean basin is the Pacific Ocean.		
42. The city of Austin is the capital of Texas.		
43. The capital of Cuba is Havana.		
44. An archipelago is a chain of islands.		
45. A lagoon is a shallow body of water between a reef and the shore.		
46. The largest freshwater lake in the world is Lake Superior. It is bordered by Ontario, Minnesota, Wisconsin, and Michigan.		
47. The Nile River is the longest river in the world at 4,160 miles.		
48. The highest waterfall in the world (979 meters) is Angel Falls in Venezuela.		
49. Epistemology is the study of knowledge and justified belief.		
50. Ghana was formerly called the Gold Coast.		
51. Hawaii was formerly known as the Sandwich Islands.		
52. Cuba's currency is the peso.		
53. In ancient math, the Roman numeral "X" means "10."		
54. Aristotle developed the theory of causality: the relation between an event, the cause, and a second event, the effect, where the second event is understood as a consequence of the first.		

	True	False
55. In chemistry, Na stands for sodium in the periodic table.	___	___
56. Tulips and baby's breath are examples of perennial plants (live more than two years).	___	___
57. CO_2 is the chemical symbol for carbon dioxide, a colorless, odorless gas.	___	___
58. Steel products can be recycled repeatedly without loss of strength.	___	___
59. A Geiger counter measures radioactive emissions.	___	___
60. Birthstone (gemstone) colors vary by the month. Are the following associations correct?	___	___

January	garnet (dark red by variable)
February	amethyst (purple)
March	aquamarine (light blue-green), bloodstone (dark green/red spots)
April	diamond
May	emerald (green)
June	alexandrite, pearl, moonstone (green)
July	ruby (red)
August	peridot (light green), sardonyx (green)
September	sapphire (blue)
October	opal (white), tourmaline (iridescent display of colors)
November	citrine (yellow to brown), topaz
December	turquoise, zircon (greenish blue), tanzanite, light blue topaz

	True	False
61. Longitude is the geographic angular distance east or west of the prime meridian.	___	___
62. Humans belong to the Homo sapiens species; the class is known as Mammalia.	___	___

	True	False
63. A prime number is any number greater than one that can only be factored by itself and the number one.		
64. One year has 52 weeks or 8,760 hours.		
65. Most years have 365 days or 525,600 minutes.		
66. One mile equals 5,280 feet or 1,760 yards.		
67. One kilogram equals 1,000 grams or 2.2046 pounds.		
68. Isaac Newton was the "father of the study of physics."		
69. The chemistry pH scale ranges from 0 to 14 and measures how acidic or basic (alkaline) a substance is. A pH of 7 is neutral. A pH less than 7 is acidic. A pH greater than 7 is basic.		
70. According to Fahrenheit the freezing temperature of water is 32 degrees and the boiling point is 212 degrees.		
71. $18 \div 2 = 9$ and $9 \times 2 = 18$.		
72. Any number multiplied by zero equals zero.		
73. Not all brain cells are alike. There are as many as ten thousand specific types of neurons in the brain.		
74. One kilometer equals 0.62 miles.		
75. France is divided into departments, Canada into provinces, and the USA into states.		

	True	False

76. There are 206 bones in the adult human body, 46 chromosomes, and 32 teeth. _____ _____

77. The 1813 Louisiana Purchase was the acquisition by the United States of France's claim to the Louisiana Territory. _____ _____

78. Alaska was purchased in 1867 by the United States. _____ _____

79. Anniversary gifts vary by the year. Are the following associations correct (traditional/modern)? _____ _____

   1 paper/clocks
   2 cotton/china
   3 leather/crystal or glass
   4 fruit or flowers/appliances
   5 wood/silverware
   6 candy or iron/wood
   7 wool or copper/desk sets
   8 pottery or bronze/linens or lace
   9 pottery/leather
   10 tin or aluminum/diamond jewelry
   15 crystal/watches
   20 china/platinum
   30 pearl/diamond
   40 ruby/ruby
   50 gold/gold
   60 diamond/diamond

80. The skin is the largest organ in the body; the femur is the longest bone. _____ _____

	True	False

81. Are the following measurement associations correct?

photometer	light
barometer	atmospheric pressure
audiometer	sound
galvanometer	electrical connection
anemometer	wind speed
bolometer	radiant energy/radiation
densitometer film	darkness of photographic or semitransparent material
calorie	energy heat
sphygmomanometer	blood pressure
manometer	pressure

82. The largest seas include the Coral, Arabian, Mediterranean, and Bering.

83. In poetry a sonnet is fourteen lines and a haiku is three lines.

84. In baseball there are nine players, in basketball there are five players, and in football there are eleven players.

85. Award cups in sports include the World Cup in soccer, the Stanley Cup in hockey, and the America's Cup in yachting.

86. The human body temperature is 98.6 degrees F (Fahrenheit) or 37 degrees C (Celsius).

87. The White House is located at 1600 Pennsylvania Avenue; the British prime minister lives at 10 Downing Street.

	True	False
88. Various organisms can invade the body. Are the following associations correct?	___	___

amoebic dysentery	protozoan parasite
chicken pox	virus
Rocky Mountain Spotted Fever	rickettsia bacteria
strep throat	bacteria

	True	False
89. Learning new things produces physical changes in the brain structure. These changes can be seen on MRI scans.	___	___
90. The capacity of short-term memory is limited to about seven items for twenty to thirty seconds. It can be stretched by using memory strategies such as chunking.	___	___
91. The largest desert is the Sahara (3.5 million square miles) in northern Africa.	___	___
92. In the grading of meat, "prime" is the best; "choice" is next.	___	___
93. Myopia is nearsightedness; hyperopia is far-sightedness.	___	___
94. On a ship, the front is the bow, the rear is the stern, the right side is starboard, and the left side is port.	___	___
95. Are the following sports categories correct?	___	___

bat-and-ball games	baseball, cricket
racquet-and-ball games	tennis, squash, racquetball
hand-and-ball-striking games	handball, 4 square
goal games	basketball, football, hockey, lacrosse
net games	volleyball
target games	bowling, lot ball

	True	False
96. Richter measures the magnitude of earthquakes; Mohs measures the hardness of solid objects.	___	___
97. Are the following associations correct?	___	___

Land of the Rising Sun   Japan
Seine River   France
Thames River   England
Andes   South America
Alps   Europe

98. The lowest ranked officer in the army is a second lieutenant, whereas the lowest in the navy is an ensign. A general wears stars, a colonel wears an eagle, a major wears an oak leaf, and a sergeant wears stripes.   ___ ___

99. Are the following associations correct?   ___ ___

Chicago   Midway
Boston   Logan
Washington   Dulles
Hartford   Bradley
Las Vegas   McCarran

100. Are the following numbers correct?   ___ ___
Seven months have thirty-one days; four months have thirty days (April, June, September, and November). February has twenty-eight days except every fourth/leap year.

Five Things to Try This Week

Although they appear to be simple, the following are designed to exercise specific cognitive functions of your brain.

- ☐ Learn more about something that interests you. (Education increases dendritic fields in the cortical language area.)

- ☐ Read something mentally stimulating at least thirty minutes daily (novels, books about hobbies and special interests, newspapers for current events). Occasionally read out loud.

- ☐ Create a more stimulating environment at home.

- ☐ Take new routes when you drive or go for walks.

- ☐ Spend more time with friends for stimulating social interactions.

Make Willpower Work for You

God created you with a will—an ability to choose. This is key. With your willpower, you can continually move toward balanced, healthy behaviors such as physical and mental exercise, a nutritious diet, and spiritual growth.

But before you can achieve and enjoy this balance, you may have some unhealthy behaviors that need to be limited or stopped. Do you drink too much alcohol, smoke, take drugs, lack sleep, rarely exercise, or overeat? Maybe you need to practice some "won't power" too. These common lifestyle challenges require a personal act of will, a personal choice, to overcome.

Do you argue with yourself when it comes to problems of will-power? It's in our nature.

As a medical doctor for over forty years, I've repeatedly seen people move toward better choices because of willpower. The choice factor is significant in their overall well-being. I've seen people choose to stop addictions, focus better, eat more appropriately, become less depressed, and act more appropriately. They often receive caring help to do so, but the choice is theirs. Sometimes willpower can reign over stress factors and, to a degree, even genetics and disease symptoms.

I'm not saying that stress and other epigenetic factors (external modifications to DNA that turn genes on or off) aren't important. I'm not saying that medical factors in the genome are unimportant. I'm saying that choices can be a significant factor in moving toward self-improvement and better health, as well as a healthier and happier outlook.

Training your brain to receive and act on the suggestion of your willpower takes practice. Part of the challenge will be to overcome bouts of doubt and a constant barrage of distractions. These obstacles will challenge your willpower every day. Without a reasonable plan, a personal commitment, and even a support system or accountability partner, there's little chance for lasting improvement.

I had a former neighbor who lacked self-discipline and willpower in his personal life. He functioned at work but was stymied by bad habits and apathy at home. He was disorganized, left home projects unfinished, and had no desire to try anything new or challenging. His children were grown, and his wife had passed away. His mental and physical health declined, but he refused medical care. Lonely and depressed, he passed away after a brief illness.

You may know someone like this. But even people like him can find new hope through developing their willpower. It's the basis for good health, a balanced lifestyle, and personal success.

It's not easy to gain power over bad habits and unhealthy desires. Did you know that it usually takes about twenty-one days to establish a habit? Beyond that point, it becomes easier and even more entrenched as it is repeated.

It's also not easy to change or manage our core personality traits. The way we think and act is partly influenced by the brain's structures, hormones, neurotransmitters, and patterns of brain activity. Sometimes our natural personality traits are positive assets; sometimes they're stumbling blocks. But what's important is that we aim to develop the positive traits and overcome the negative ones.

Scripture Power

In addition to your choices and willpower, there is a mighty power available to help you on your journey. I'll tell you about one of the most powerful forces on earth—power not only in the spiritual world but also in the intellectual world. Power that has protected me. Power that is both pragmatic and abstract. Power I simply call "Scripture Power."

It is much more than intellectual. I've seen this power work in my life in different ways: direct empowerment by God, direction, discipline, discernment, diversion from sin, increased intellectual ability, joy, and correction, to name just a few.

The Bible is the number-one-selling book of all time, the greatest book ever written. The Bible is not of this world, it is "God-breathed." When I reflect on God's Word, I think about its rich history—it's still inerrant, infallible, and inalienable after thousands of years. God was the author through forty human writers; sixty-six books are miraculously one book. This timeless Scripture ranges from the history of humankind, to relevance for today, to hope for tomorrow.

Although the accounts of people in the Bible were divinely inspired, the individuals were mere mortals with similar strengths, weaknesses, and personal struggles we experience today. We can identify with them and learn lessons from their lives that help us cope with the stresses of the twenty-first century.

The societies in which these biblical characters lived were vastly different from ours—no technology or mass transportation and limited scientific knowledge. They didn't face such things as the threat of nuclear warfare, but their timely concerns were as real to them as ours are to us. They grappled with similar life-and-death issues. Accounts of their lives and how God works in and among us provide lessons that can guide our choices today.

The Bible teaches both individual choice and God's sovereignty. Choice and sovereignty don't negate each other. God wants us to make good choices; this book can guide you through some of them.

Warm-Up Vocabulary Quiz

The brain can comprehend a one-word definition better than a long one, so definitions are best kept short. It's usually not enough to just read through a list of new words with their definitions and try to remember them. Once you learn the correct definitions, review them over a period of two weeks to help store the words in your permanent memory. This also aids neuroplasticity.

Circle the correct definition for the words below. Research the correct answer if you are unsure, then say it aloud and use the word in a sentence.

1. abide
   A. to leave
   B. to love
   C. to remain/wait
   D. to persuade

2. bamboozle
   A. to prohibit
   B. to deceive
   C. to defer/delay
   D. to lull/soothe

3. caveat
   A. warning
   B. encouragement
   C. cave
   D. conclave

4. decry
   A. to welcome
   B. to detain
   C. to design
   D. to denounce

5. doff
   A. to take off/remove
   B. to put on
   C. to drink
   D. to dote/love

6. descry
   A. decry/denounce
   B. catch sight of something
   C. cry
   D. hopeless

7. catamaran
    A. cat
    B. dictator
    C. raft
    D. matron
8. proffer
    A. to rescind
    B. to poke
    C. to offer
    D. to play
9. trek
    A. to trick
    B. to trespass
    C. to travel
    D. to argue
10. wily
    A. weary/tired
    B. cunning/sly
    C. mean
    D. wild

Know Your Words 1

Learn these one-word definitions for seven words.

Even if you already know some of the following words, practice using them more often in conversations.

Review new words over a period of weeks to help store them in your permanent memory.

abash: to embarrass
abate: to reduce
aberrant: atypical
abet: to aid
abide: to remain
abject: sad
abridge: to shorten

Puzzle Power 1

Fact: Increasing mental exercise improves cognition.

The more years you consistently stimulate your memory the better chance you have of reducing the threat of cognitive decline or dementia. If you are thirty years old and start right now, you may be able to accomplish years or decades of preventive care. Investing this effort for a vital mind is similar to the money you're already investing for a comfortable retirement lifestyle. Try the following mental exercises.

A man is looking at a portrait on a wall and says, "Brothers and sisters I have none, but this man's father is my father's son." At whose portrait is he looking?[1]

Memorization

Memorize the forty-six US presidents in order. List them as quickly as you can and repeat them daily: Washington, Adams, Jefferson, Madison, Monroe, Adams, Jackson, Van Buren, Harrison, Tyler, Polk, Taylor, Fillmore, Pierce, Buchanan, Lincoln, Johnson, Grant, Hayes, Garfield, Arthur, Cleveland, Harrison, Cleveland, McKinley, Roosevelt, Taft, Wilson, Harding, Coolidge, Hoover, Roosevelt, Truman, Eisenhower, Kennedy, Johnson, Nixon, Ford, Carter, Reagan, Bush, Clinton, Bush, Obama, Trump, Biden.

When you've mastered that, try learning and practicing them in reverse order: Biden, Trump, Obama, Bush, Clinton, Bush, Reagan, Carter, Ford, Nixon, Johnson, Kennedy, Eisenhower, Truman, Roosevelt, Hoover, Coolidge, Harding, Wilson, Taft, Roosevelt, McKinley, Cleveland, Harrison, Cleveland, Arthur, Garfield, Hayes, Grant, Johnson, Lincoln, Buchanan, Pierce, Fillmore, Taylor, Polk, Tyler, Harrison, Van Buren, Jackson, Adams, Monroe, Madison, Jefferson, Adams, Washington.

If you're not interested in learning the presidents, make a list of thirty to forty items in a topic that relates to your profession or hobbies and memorize that list.

Math Exercises

Practice math exercises in your head when you go for a walk or while you wait in the car.

Calculating tips for staff at restaurants, airports, hotels, beauty shops, and other places is a daily challenge. Impress your friends and ditch your smartphone calculator.

Find 10 percent of the total bill by moving the decimal to the left one space.

5 percent is half that amount.

For 15 percent, add the 10 and 5 percent.

20 percent is double the 10 percent.

Example: Your bill is $148.00. Round it up to $150.00.

10 percent is $15.00.

20 percent is 2 x $15 = $30.00 for the tip.

(Of course, you can adjust the amount up or down.)

In your head, add or subtract serial numbers (2s, 3s, 4s, etc.) from 100 as quickly as possible. Then choose a number to multiply by itself. Start with smaller numbers like 2s, 3s, and 4s to warm up, then progress to 7s, 8s, and 9s. Repeat the series daily until you can do it quickly. Then move to a new series.

Memory Boosters through Entertainment

☐ Play board games, chess, and cards; do puzzles.

☐ Play video games or explore the internet on topics of interest.

☐ Listen to music and learn the lyrics to new songs.

☐ Take a free class at a local library or college.

Change Your Routines

- Comb your hair and brush your teeth with the opposite hand.
- Take ten- to fifteen-minute power naps. (Brains at rest can help organize information and memories.)
- Do stretching exercises during television commercials.
- Make changes in the order of daily routines.
- Focus on five items in a room, then try to recall those items throughout the day, especially when you have changed to a different location.

Now ask yourself: Do I honestly feel that my routines and choices are healthy? Would the people I trust say my actions and choices are healthy?

Debunking Common Myths about the Brain

New research is correcting a few popular misbeliefs.[2]

Some literature and advertisements still claim that *we use only 10 percent of our brain*. This is untrue. Actually, almost every part of the brain is active most of the time.

It's all downhill after age thirty. It's true that some cognitive skills decline as we age, but some actually improve such as wisdom, vocabulary, managing emotions, better perspective, patience, and knowing our life's purpose.

There's a history of likening the brain to the most advanced technology. The most common is that *the brain is like a computer*: its processing speed, storage capacity, parallel circuits, inputs, and outputs. But the metaphor is a poor comparison. The brain is not hardwired like a computer. It doesn't have a set memory capacity that's waiting to be filled up, and it doesn't perform computations the way a computer does. We actively interpret, anticipate, and pay attention to different elements of the world. The brain is actually quite "moldable" (brain plasticity is the process in which the brain's neural synapses and pathways are altered as an effect of environmental, behavioral, and neural changes), unlike a computer.

Sneezing kills brain cells. It doesn't.

Normal aging kills brain cells. For years, it was believed that brain cells start dying around age thirty. But recent studies have determined that brain cells actually continue to develop in certain parts of the brain.[3] However, just like the rest of the body they do undergo changes because of adapting to new experiences. Age may cause a decreased number of synapses between cells. There may also be changes that disable some chemicals that communicate between cells. Neurodegenerative diseases like Alzheimer's do kill brain cells, but normal aging doesn't cause a downhill spiral.[4] It's comforting to know that some of our brain cells aren't disappearing with every birthday. They won't quit on us if we do everything we can to care for them.

Some of us are predominately right-brained and others are more left-brained. This concept might have come from Roger Sperry's studies[5] in 1967 that some functions of the left and right cerebral hemispheres are different. He concluded that the left brain is more logical, analytical, and mathematical; and the right brain is more focused on intuition, creativity, sensory input, and synthesis of information.

The speculation was that many scientists, physicians, and accountants are left-brained, while artists and composers are probably right-brained. In current research, conclusions are more complex. The evidence from more than one thousand brain scans shows no actual signs of consistent left or right dominance.[6] The key is the way the parts interact, not each part by itself. We need to work on developing both sides of our brains.

Listening to classical music (the "Mozart effect") makes babies smarter.[7] It's been proven this is not the case.

We need to drink a lot of water to make our brains function better. While this is not true, drinking water does help maintain the balance of body fluids, which benefits digestion, absorption, circulation, maintenance of body temperature, and transporting nutrients. (The adult human body overall is composed of about 60 percent water.)

Be Aware of Early Warning Signs

A person experiencing cognitive decline may have trouble with some of the following symptoms. Do you notice any of these in yourself, a family member, or a close friend?

- forget things more often
- forget appointments or social events
- lose your train of thought in conversations
- feel increasingly overwhelmed by making decisions, planning tasks, or following instructions
- have trouble finding your way around familiar environments
- act impulsively or show increasingly poor judgment
- have trouble learning new information

Make a List

Order guides our personal, social, and professional lives. Rules, systems, networks, customs, and values guide our behaviors. We even use order in our attire, sports, dining, daily routines, and relationships.

But this sense of order can sometimes get off balance due to circumstances or medical conditions. For example, if a person is confined and deprived of normal sights and sounds for an extended time, the brain and emotions can get distorted. In loneliness, people may give inanimate objects human-like qualities. When the brain feels disorder in stressful situations, it may distort memories or reasoning, which harms relationships, productivity, emotions, and thinking. The elderly and chronically ill are particularly susceptible to these complications.

Our brains also like *lists* because information is organized and condensed, and they make immediate understanding and later recall easier. We're naturally drawn to lists because of our natural human tendency to categorize things. Our minds are used to lists because we use them in our everyday lives; even the one billion websites in our current reach are based on list formats.

I encourage you to make lists. (Here I go again . . .) Lists can help you

- remember things
- bring order to your life
- simplify and clarify

- focus
- relieve stress
- avoid procrastinating

Use them. Review them. Update them. Let them guide you.

Historical Characters

What were these people known for in history? Are all the following associations correct?

Even one wrong fact (date, association) renders the entire statement false.

		True	False
Socrates (470–399 BC)	wisdom	____	____
Cleopatra (69–30 BC)	beauty	____	____
Caligula, Roman Emperor (AD 12–41)	depravity	____	____
Attila the Hun (died in AD 453)	"the scourge of God"	____	____
Oliver Cromwell (1599–1658)	purity	____	____
Peter the Great of Russia (1672–1725)	large stature	____	____
Elizabeth the Great of Russia (1709–62)	promiscuity	____	____
Napoleon (1769–1821)	small stature	____	____
Abraham Lincoln (1809–65)	honesty	____	____
Martin Luther King Jr. (1929–68)	civil rights	____	____

History of Ideas

This historical research deals with the expression, preservation, and change of human ideas over time. It may involve the histories of philosophy, science, or literature.

Is the following sequence of ideas in correct chronological order? True or false? Some dates are approximations.

		True (correct)	False (incorrect)
c. 3200 BC	Earliest system of writing, the cuneiform alphabet, was formed.	_____	_____
c. 2000 BC	Mathematics started.	_____	_____
507 BC	Democracy began in Athens, Greece.	_____	_____
AD 321	Emperor Constantine changed the Roman week to seven days, and Sunday became an official day of rest.	_____	_____
300–700	Gunpowder was developed by the Chinese.	_____	_____
1215	The jury system was developed in King John's England (Magna Carta).	_____	_____
c. 1400	Gutenberg developed the printing press.	_____	_____

		True (correct)	False (incorrect)
c. 1540	Copernicus published the concept of the earth revolving around the sun every twenty-four hours.	_____	_____
c. 1663	Otto von Guericke developed the electrostatic generator.	_____	_____
1687	Isaac Newton developed the gravity concept of the physical universe.	_____	_____
c. 1740	John Harrison developed the concept of longitude, helping navigators.	_____	_____
1760	Industrial Revolution gained momentum.	_____	_____
1792	Mary Wollstonecraft's *A Vindication of the Rights of Women* was published.	_____	_____
1837–39	Photography was invented by Daguerre and Talbot.	_____	_____
1848	Karl Marx described socialism in the *Communist Manifesto*.	_____	_____
c. 1860	Louis Pasteur proved the relationship between germs and diseases.	_____	_____
1856–65	Gregor Mendes discovered genetic inheritance.	_____	_____
1903	The Wright brothers operated a flying machine at Kitty Hawk, North Carolina.	_____	_____

		True (correct)	False (incorrect)
1905	Einstein's Theory of Special Relativity, his equation $E=MC^2$, and thoughts that preceded the atomic bomb were delivered.	_____	_____
1913	Henry Ford's first assembly line started.	_____	_____
1941	World War II, Fascism, Hitler, and Japan exerted influence and power at Pearl Harbor.	_____	_____
1947	Television invaded living rooms in the USA.	_____	_____
1936	Electronic computers started with Alan Turing, founder of modern computing.	_____	_____
1975	Animal rights grew with Peter Singer's *Animal Liberation*.	_____	_____
1984	The search for extraterrestrial intelligence was launched.	_____	_____
1989	The World Wide Web was started by Sir Tim Berners-Lee.	_____	_____
2005	Eris was discovered, 27 percent larger than Pluto and ninth largest body to orbit the sun.	_____	_____
2010	An aging gene was discovered that may make it possible to increase life spans and delay certain degenerative diseases.	_____	_____

Know Your Words 2

Learn these definitions for seven words.

Even if you already know some of the following words, practice using them more often in conversations.

Review new words over a period of weeks to help store them in your permanent memory.

bailiwick: area of skill
ballyhoo: blatant advertising
banal: commonplace
bantam: small
bathos: overly sentimental
batten: to thrive
befuddle: to confuse thoroughly

Puzzle Power 2

Are you able to interpret the following mental puzzle? If not, don't feel bad—few can. Solving it takes deeper thinking than many readily attain on a daily basis.

> A traveler is on her way to Delhi when she comes to a fork in the road. She is wondering which way to go when two men appear. One cannot tell the truth, and the other cannot tell a lie. The traveler doesn't know which is which. What *one* question can she ask which will show her the right road to Delhi?[8]

Brace Yourself for the Aging Process

Normal aging involves *biological changes* in the central nervous system, brain cells, and body chemicals.

Neurological changes—the gradual decline in the blood flow to the brain—can affect metabolism, sleep patterns, and parts of the nervous system. They may eventually slow reflexes and affect balance. The brain doesn't send or process nerve impulses as well or as quickly. Mental changes happen at different rates and intensities for each person. Some brain functions may remain stable while other functions decline.

It gets harder to lose weight, and skin loses elasticity. Joints, muscles, teeth, blood circulation, digestion, and immune systems begin to show their age.

Physical activities decline with the loss of muscle strength, muscle mass, and flexibility. Some motor dysfunctions may predict a later onset of Alzheimer's and cognitive decline.

Less air is taken in with each breath, and the *lungs* don't absorb as much oxygen.

The *senses* aren't spared either. Age-related dry mouth, dry eyes, and hearing loss are common. The eyes react more slowly to changes in light, and glaucoma and cataracts develop. High-pitched sounds are particularly hard for the elderly to hear.

Eating problems result from less sensitive taste buds, decreased sense of smell, and difficulty chewing and swallowing.

More noticeably, *good looks* are lost. Hair thins and turns gray, dry skin wrinkles and heals more slowly, and body fat gets redistributed.

There is a general decline in the function of *internal organs and systems* and an increase in illnesses such as diabetes, heart disease, hypertension, and cancer.

Testosterone and estrogen *hormone levels* also diminish, which can produce age-related sexual dysfunction.

Stress affects the quality of relationships. Losses, fears, and boredom increase.

Energy levels depend more on lifestyle and attitude than chronological age. Good nutrition, restful sleep, and regular exercise can help keep energy levels high.

With advancing age, *psychological problems* can set in. There is often a decline in self-esteem because of dependency and a narrowing of interests. Friendships can fade when unhealthy coping defenses surface, such as withdrawing and giving up.

Depression is the most common mental disorder in the vulnerable elderly. Typical symptoms include sadness, health-related and bodily function worries, sleep disturbance, loss of appetite, low energy, and back pain. Emotions are easily triggered, and judgment is compromised.

But all of this doesn't mean you have to give up or be cranky in your senior years. Happiness is a choice just like preserving your memory is a choice. You can make every stage of life fulfilling, peaceful, and productive if you choose. It's encouraging to know that Benjamin Franklin, Albert Schweitzer, Winston Churchill, and Michelangelo made their major contributions in their eighties.

Abraham Lincoln said it well: "Most people are about as happy as they choose to be." Some studies have determined that happiness may decline in the first few decades of adulthood, but it often upswings again later. Life satisfaction typically dips when people are in their forties and then increases as they reach their sixties, which is good news for seniors. A 2011 study from Stanford University concluded that peak emotional life may not actually occur until the seventh decade.[9] An anonymous individual testifies to this:

> There is great freedom that comes with aging. I know I'm some-times forgetful. But some of life is just as well forgotten. Eventually, I remember the important things. I am so blessed to have lived long enough to have my youthful laughs etched into grooves on my face. As you get older, it is easier to be positive. You care less about what other people think. I like being old.[10]

United States Government Quiz

The government of the United States is the federal government of the republic of fifty states, as well as one capital district and several territories. The full name of the republic is United States of America. No other name appears in the Constitution.

Are all of the following statements correct? (All of the details must be accurate for a true rating.)

	True	False
1. The number of US senators is 100.	___	___
2. The number of US representatives is 435.	___	___
3. The number of Supreme Court justices is 9.	___	___
4. United States senators serve unlimited six-year terms. United States representatives serve unlimited two-year terms.	___	___
5. The amendment to the US Constitution that gave women the right to vote was the Nineteenth Amendment.	___	___
6. The three branches of government are executive (president and fifteen departments), judicial (courts), and legislative (Senate and House of Representatives).	___	___

	True	False
7. Medicare started in 1965.	_____	_____
8. The national government cannot change state boundaries.	_____	_____
9. Congress can override the president's veto of a bill.	_____	_____
10. A probate court is for matters involving wills, estates, and guardianship of children.	_____	_____

United States Constitution Quiz

The Preamble to the US Constitution states:

> We the People of the United States, in Order to form a more perfect Union, establish Justice, insure domestic Tranquility, provide for the common defense, promote the general Welfare, and secure the Blessings of Liberty to ourselves and our Posterity, do ordain and establish this Constitution for the United States of America.

Are the following statements correct? (All of the details must be accurate for a true rating.)

	Amendment	True	False
1	freedom of speech, religion, assembly, and press	___	___
2	right to bear arms	___	___
4	prohibits unreasonable search and seizure	___	___
5	right to due process; no testifying against self	___	___
6	right to fair, speedy, public trial	___	___
7	right to jury trial	___	___
8	prohibits cruel or excessive punishment	___	___

	Amendment	True	False
10	limits powers of federal government	___	___
13	abolishes slavery	___	___
14	defines citizenship	___	___
15	prohibits denial of the right to vote based on race, color, or previous condition of servitude	___	___
16	allows federal government to collect income tax	___	___
19	women's right to vote	___	___
26	voting age eighteen years	___	___

Historical Ages

BC—Before Christ

(BCE—Before Common Era)

AD—Anno Domini (in the year of the Lord); After Death of Christ

(CE—Common Era)

Circa—approximately or about (c., ca., circ., cca.)

Ancient history (3600 BC–AD 500)

Postclassical Era (500–1500)

Modern history (1500–present)

Is the following sequence of time correct? True or false? The dates may be approximations.

		True (correct)	False (incorrect)
Ends c. 6000 BC–2000 BC	Stone Age	____	____
c. 3000 BC–1500 BC	Bronze Age	____	____
c. 1200 BC–AD 300	Iron Age	____	____
c. 500–1500	Dark Ages and Middle Ages	____	____
c. 1300–1600	Renaissance and Reformation	____	____

		True (correct)	False (incorrect)
c. 1600–1700	Age of Enlightenment	____	____
1776	Declaration of Independence (USA)	____	____
1861–65	Civil War	____	____
1914–18	World War I	____	____
1939–45	World War II	____	____
1948	Israel became a nation again	____	____
1954–68	Civil Rights Movement	____	____
1980	Internet global system of computer networks	____	____
1991	World Wide Web available to the public	____	____
2001	World Trade Center destroyed (USA)	____	____
1975, 1982, 1991, 2008	Recent global recessions	____	____

Historical Personalities

These historical figures are from a range of cultures and countries. Are there any mistakes in the following information?

	True	False
1. Alexander the Great was the king of Macedonia and conqueror of Greece and Persia by 325 BC. He was taught by Aristotle, who was taught by Plato, who was taught by Socrates.	___	___
2. Cleopatra was the queen of Egypt in 51 BC.	___	___
3. Julius Caesar was betrayed by Brutus in 44 BC.	___	___
4. The Allies fought together to defeat the Germans and other Axis countries (Japan, Italy) in World War II (1939–45).	___	___
5. Benedict Arnold was a traitor in the American Revolution in 1780.	___	___
6. Napoleon Bonaparte was the French emperor defeated in the Battle of Waterloo in 1815.	___	___
7. John Wilkes Booth assassinated President Abraham Lincoln in 1865.	___	___
8. Custer was defeated by Sitting Bull in the Battle of Little Bighorn in 1876.	___	___

	True	False
9. Adolf Hitler was the leader of Germany during World War II.	____	____
10. Winston Churchill was the prime minister of Britain during World War II (1939–45) and again from 1951–55.	____	____
11. $E=MC^2$ is the correlation between mass and energy (E is units of energy, M is units of mass, C^2 is the speed of light squared or multiplied by itself).	____	____
12. Thomas Edison, 1847–1931, patented over one thousand inventions.	____	____

Music and Memory

do, re, mi, fa, so, la, ti, do

There are strong correlations between music and academic achievement. Other musical values include artistic, aesthetic, practical, social, entertainment, therapeutic, self-affirmation, and economic benefits.

Is the following information about music events and/or musicians correct? Answer true or false concerning the time sequence and all the facts. (Dates may be approximations.)

		True	False
c. 1000 BC	Medieval period: mostly Christian music survived	____	____
c. AD 1500	Renaissance: humanistic music	____	____
c. 1700	Baroque with intensity: Bach's *Mass in B Minor*, Handel's *Messiah*, and Vivaldi's *Four Seasons* Opera is an example.	____	____
c. 1800	Classical with balance in music: Mozart's *The Marriage of Figaro*, Beethoven's *Symphony No. 9*, and Haydn's symphonies and concertos	____	____

		True	False
c. 1850 Romantic period with emotional feelings emphasized	Beethoven's *Moonlight Sonata* was a bridge to this period. Chopin—the "poet of the piano"	____	____
c. 1860	Nationalism with a patriotic flavor: "Dixie" and "Battle Hymn of the Republic"	____	____
c. 1900	Neoclassical period (jazz, folk songs): Copland's *Appalachian Spring* and Stravinsky's *Firebird*	____	____
c. 1900	Expressionism with harmony distortion for expressive effect: Schoenberg's *Pierrot Lunaire*	____	____
c. 1900	Impressionism with focus on emotions: Debussy's "Clair de Lune" and prelude to the "Afternoon of a Faun"	____	____
c. 1930	Modernism with diverse musical styles; no dominant music genre	____	____
c. 1980	Postmodernism, a continuation of electronic and diverse music: Michael Jackson, King of Pop	____	____

Judgment Exercises

Judgment is the ability to make considered decisions or come to sensible conclusions. It is discernment, common sense, perception, wisdom, sharpness, reasoning, acuity, and astuteness.

Judgment can decrease with decreased cognition and memory. Work to keep your judgment skills sharp. For example, if you were in a theater and someone yelled, "Fire," what would you do (in order of preference)?

Now, consider a more difficult scenario. If you found a letter on the street with an address on it, what would you do?

Conceptual Exercises

Conceptual exercises help us develop approaches to how we understand the dynamics of people, science, technology, and the environment. Increasing the ability to work with conceptual problems and relationships can boost brainpower.

Following are analogical examples. Can you identify the relationships?

Contrast:	*hot/cold/sharp/_____*	a. dull b. cutting c. acute d. keen
Similar, contrast:	*ecstatic/happy/sad/* _____	a. melancholic b. glad c. ecstatic d. euphoric
Part, whole:	*hour/day/day/_____*	a. week b. second c. minute d. millisecond
Whole, part:	*USA/Washington, DC/* *Russia/_____*	a. Moscow b. Bern c. Madrid d. Rome
Type of:	*insect/arthropod/lobster/* _____	a. crustacean b. mollusk c. oyster d. squid

Completion:	*Mexico/City/New York/_____*	a. City b. New York c. New Jersey d. USA
Implicit relationship:	*states/USA/provinces/_____*	a. Canada b. France c. Switzerland d. England
Sound alike:	*Hi/Bye/now/_____*	a. how b. then c. good d. future
Verb tenses:	*come/came/go/_____*	a. went b. got c. bye d. get
Letters reversed:	*CAT/TAC/DO/_____*	a. OD b. DID c. DON'T d. GONE
Example:	*mom/palindrome/bark/_____*	a. onomatopoeia b. semantics c. homonym d. antediluvian
Mathematical equivalents:	*>/greater than/</_____*	a. less than b. equal c. forget d. abstract
Mathematical opposites:	*>/<* greater than/_____	a. less than b. equal to c. unequal d. ordinal number

Bad, Good, Better, Best— You Decide

You may be thinking, "I'd like to make better choices. It seems harder than when I was growing up because now there are more opportunities and options, and the consequences seem more complex. How do I know if my choices are right? Should I follow my head or my heart?" Needless to say, we can't keep flying by the seat of our pants.

Note which of the following tips would be helpful in your circumstances:

Be clear on your *personal values*. Every choice has a consequence. Make sure your decisions are aligned with your moral and spiritual values.

Repeated choices become habits. Habits make you the person you are. Over time, good choices and bad choices become habits that are hard to break. The neural pathways become automatic. How do you break a bad habit like knuckle cracking or nail-biting? (1) Notice when you're doing it and why. Is it because of stress or boredom? (2) Keep a written tally of each time you do it. You may be surprised how often it is. (3) When you catch yourself, make a conscious effort to resist, relax, and distract. Replace it with a good behavior.

Having choices in the first place can be a *motivating factor to do the right thing*. You rarely have to make a choice between obvious good and evil, but you can identify when there is a difference between what you *want* to do and what you *should* do.

The great thing about choices is that you *almost always have more chances* to turn things around if you're going in a wrong direction. The key is to acknowledge it and make a change.

Improve relationships with your family and build a *good support system*. Ask people you trust for advice in your decision-making processes. You have the power to over-haul bad situations through better choices.

Don't let poor choices from the past keep you from making better choices now. *Learn from past mistakes* and suc-cesses. Poor choices can lower your self-esteem. Today is a blank slate; start fresh.

Spend more *time on things that matter* instead of wasting so much time on things that don't. Stay aware of what you're doing and if it fits in with your *long-term goals*. A long-term perspective will likely lead you to better decisions.

Some choices have immediate *consequences*; others may take longer to reward or hurt you. What are some other op-tions or alternatives? Think about the worst and the best things that could happen if you make a certain decision. Are you willing to live with the risks?

Think about whether your choices *benefit or harm others* who may be involved.

Make decisions with both your *head and heart*. Be logical but also be aware of your gut instincts.

God uses *guilt* to influence you to change your mind when you're doing something wrong. If you feel guilty, make changes.

Making decisions is a *lifelong skill*.

Your daily choices, habits, and willingness to move past failures will direct your days. *Choose well.*

Know Your Words 3

Learn these definitions for seven words.

Even if you already know some of the following words, practice using them more often in conversations.

Review new words over a period of weeks to help store them in your permanent memory.

maverick: an independent person

meager: small amount

meander: to wander casually

melee: a free-for-all

menagerie: a group of animals

mendacious: dishonest

methodical: systematic

Explorers' Passions and Purpose

By knowing our forerunners, we are reminded who we are. Consider how these explorers followed their passions. The following facts are in chronological order, but are all the facts true?

Make an extra effort to commit these facts to memory. Amaze your friends and family by dropping this information into conversations.

	True (correct)	False (incorrect)
1. Eric the Red discovered Greenland in 982.	____	____
2. Leif Erikson and his Vikings discovered Newfoundland in 1000.	____	____
3. Marco Polo traveled to China in 1271.	____	____
4. Bartolomeu Dias sailed around the southern tip of Africa in 1488.	____	____
5. Christopher Columbus with his small fleet (Niña, Pinta, and Santa Maria) entered the Caribbean Sea in 1492.	____	____
6. European explorers traveled to the Spice Islands (Indonesia) in the 1500s.	____	____

	True (correct)	False (incorrect)
7. Vasco Núñez de Balboa crossed Panama to see the Pacific Ocean in 1513.	____	____
8. Ponce de León searched for "The Fountain of Youth" in Florida but brought back "A Fountain of Death" (tobacco) in 1514.	____	____
9. Ferdinand Magellan sailed around the world in 1519–22.	____	____
10. Hernán Cortés conquered the Aztecs in Mexico in 1521.	____	____

Literary Classics

The classics have something for everyone, including culture, history, and philosophy. They are entertaining, enlightening, and challenging and encourage mental versatility.

Are all of the authors and their famous works correct?

		True (correct)	False (incorrect)
750 BC	Homer, *The Iliad* (about the Trojan wars; Homer is considered to be the first writer of Western literature)	_____	_____
380 BC	Plato, *Republic* (first book of Western philosophy)	_____	_____
1478	Geoffrey Chaucer, *The Canterbury Tales* (brought literature to the middle class)	_____	_____
1605/1615	Cervantes Saavedra, *Don Quixote* in two volumes (the first modern novel)	_____	_____
1667	John Milton, *Paradise Lost*	_____	_____
1697	William Shakespeare, *Romeo and Juliet* (Shakespeare is the greatest English poet and dramatist)	_____	_____

		True (correct)	False (incorrect)
1726	Jonathan Swift, *Gulliver's Travels*	____	____
1732	Benjamin Franklin, *Poor Richard's Almanac*	____	____
1813	Jane Austen, *Pride and Prejudice*	____	____
1818	Mary Shelley, *Frankenstein*	____	____
1845	Edgar Allan Poe, "The Crow"	____	____
1850	Nathaniel Hawthorne, *The Scarlet Letter*	____	____
1851	Herman Melville, *Moby-Dick*	____	____
1852	Harriet Beecher Stowe, *Uncle Tom's Cabin*	____	____
1854	Henry David Thoreau, *Walden*	____	____
1855	Walt Whitman, *Leaves of Grass* (first edition)	____	____
1860–61	Charles Dickens, *Great Expectations*	____	____
1866	Fyodor Dostoevsky, *Crime and Punishment*	____	____
1869	Leo Nikolayevich Tolstoy, *War and Peace*	____	____
1884	Mark Twain (Samuel Clemens), *Huckleberry Finn* (first edition)	____	____
1894	George Bernard Shaw, *Arms and the Man*	____	____

		True (correct)	False (incorrect)
1906	Upton Sinclair, *The Jungle*	____	____
1916	Robert Frost, "The Road Not Taken"	____	____
1922	T. S. Eliot, "The Waste Land"	____	____
1926	Sinclair Lewis, *Elmer Gantry*	____	____
1929	William Faulkner, *The Sound and the Fury*	____	____
1929	Ernest Hemingway, *A Farewell to Arms*	____	____
1939	John Steinbeck, *Grapes of Wrath*	____	____
1944	Tennessee Williams, *The Glass Menagerie*	____	____
1949	Arthur Miller, *Death of a Salesman*	____	____
1973	Aleksandr Isayevich Solzhenitsyn, *The Gulag Archipelago*	____	____
1982	Alice Walker, *The Color Purple*	____	____
1997	J. K. Rowling, *Harry Potter and the Philosopher's Stone*	____	____

Get Enough Uninterrupted Sleep

Insomnia in mid- to late life can be a serious problem. The brain generates about as much energy as a small lightbulb even during sleep, and it needs uninterrupted sleep to recuperate. Doctors often hear, "I can't sleep. Can you help me?" If you or a family member has sleep difficulties, you're not alone. About one-third of the population reports insomnia symptoms, including problems falling asleep and staying asleep. Having nonrestorative sleep can lead to daytime dysfunction.

Check the following activities that you will try for improving your quality of sleep:

☐ Avoid long-term use of sleep aid medications because they may disturb stage IV sleep, making sleep less productive.[11]

☐ Set a regular sleep routine for bedtime and wake-up time.

☐ Reduce light, noise, and stimulating activities one to two hours before bed.

☐ Avoid drinking caffeine and alcohol or eating in the four hours before bedtime.

☐ Reduce/shorten daytime naps.

☐ Exercise early in the day because it releases energy-boosting adrenaline.

☐ Clear your mind of worries.

☐ Use a fan for white noise.

☐ Read a relaxing novel or listen to music to get sleepy.

☐ Relax by taking a warm shower or bath. It can stimulate blood flow, so give yourself an hour before bed.

☐ Have a warm, decaffeinated, sugarless drink just before bedtime. (It draws blood to the stomach, causing a sleep sensation because of the slightly decreased blood flow to parts of the brain.)

☐ Check your medications for sleep-related side effects.

Exercise Physically to Get a Boost Mentally

- An active lifestyle increases the brain volume. It has been well documented that aerobic activity is a powerful stimulus for generating structural changes in the brain.
- Physical exercise increases oxygen in the bloodstream and pumps it to the brain. Oxygen is fuel for the brain and helps increase neuron activity.
- Regular exercise releases endorphins, which are natural painkillers and mood boosters, and it burns off toxic chemicals caused by stress.

A good way to kick all of this into action is to schedule yourself a break in your daily routine. For instance, climb stairs at the office or take a walk around the block with the dog or a child. Having someone join you makes it more fun.

Contrary to what many people believe, strenuous workouts aren't necessary to get the benefits of exercise or motion. Research confirms that thirty minutes of moderate activity like walking or cycling three or more times a week is preferable to working out for three hours just once a week. Other aerobic exercises are cardio machines, swimming, hiking, taking exercise classes, or dancing.

Start each day with my quick "7 × 7" wake-up routine:

7 push-ups (on your knees, if you need to)
7 sit-ups/crunches

7 straight leg lefts
7 side leg lifts
7 chest expansions (pull arms back)
7 neck stretches forward and backward
7 full body folds to touch the floor (or your toes)

Consider a Mediterranean Diet and Maintain a Healthy Weight

Everything you eat drugs your brain for good or bad so be careful what you put in your mouth.

Do you or a family member struggle with being overweight? Studies show that a body mass index (BMI) greater than twenty-five may decrease memory. The BMI is a calculated ratio of a person's height and weight. Go online for BMI charts or calculators to get your number. If you are extremely muscular, this number may be skewed higher, but it is a good gauge.

Eat less. It can't get any simpler than that. Portion size is important because mental focus is impacted by eating too much as well as too little. Use smaller plates and bowls, use doggy bags from restaurants, and enjoy every bite. A standard recommendation is to eat until you are 80 percent full. Another hint—avoid extremely low-carb diets because the brain needs a steady flow of carbohydrates to fuel it twenty-four hours a day. Do eat some protein at every meal and decrease obvious and hidden sugars (in prepackaged foods).

Eating breakfast has benefits. Some people skip breakfast to avoid the calories. But eating breakfast is a good foundation for a productive day at any age. For example, the USDA's School Breakfast Program helps foster success in the classroom and healthy lifetime habits. Research supports the claims that breakfast helps improve attention, problem-solving ability, and memory.

Eating well in general contributes to brain longevity as well as short-term benefits like learning and concentration.

I'm especially concerned about the elderly because they typically have poor eating habits, for many reasons. The brain requires certain nutrients and vitamins, so malnutrition makes this population even more vulnerable to mental decline and diseases. Keep this in mind when you visit a senior. Instead of taking flowers and candy, take them a little word-search book, a fun magazine to read, or fresh blueberries.

Wise diet choices include foods high in omega-3 fatty acids or B and D vitamins, plant-derived foods, the spice turmeric, and of course all the other healthy foods you know you should be eating. You can do an online search for specific food lists and sample menus.

Try the Mediterranean diet. Research has proven that people who eat more produce, fish, whole grains, and healthy fats not only weigh less but also have a decreased risk for heart disease, depression, and dementia.

Consider the following foods as a general guideline and make adjustments for your individual preferences. These smart-choice foods are relatively low-cost, widely available, and delicious. A basic rule: If it's white (potatoes, bread), eat less; if it's green, eat more. By making just one or two of the following diet changes, your brain will gain health.[12]

- more fish (omega-3 fatty acids)
- more vegetables (especially yellow and leafy greens)
- baked or grilled chicken and turkey
- tea and coffee in moderation
- more whole grains
- fruits (berries and those with edible skins) for fiber
- more legumes (peas, beans) and nuts (almonds)

- herbs and spices (instead of salt) to flavor foods
- coconut or olive oil (not saturated fats) for cooking to improve levels of good (HDL) cholesterol
- less cheese; choose low-fat dairy products
- less beef and pork
- less cakes, pies, and cookies; avoid simple sugars
- less fried foods
- not skipping meals (skipping meals causes your body to convert food into fat and slows metabolism)

Consider Vitamin Supplements and Antioxidants

It's a good idea to become familiar with omega-3 fatty acids, the B family of vitamins, vitamin D, and antioxidants. In general, vitamins don't hurt—they may even help in many situations. But beware of excessive use of any vitamin. A quality daily multiple vitamin supplement is probably a good idea for people who don't and can't keep up with a well-balanced daily diet.[13]

Be aware: Don't fall for health-food gimmicks that mega-vitamins touted to be "natural" are better than those synthesized in labs. A vitamin is a chemical—a chemical used in a particular biochemical reaction. It doesn't make any difference whether that chemical has been extracted naturally or synthesized in a lab.

Sometimes supplements are needed—for example, iron for anemia and vitamin D if a person does not get enough sun exposure for the body to make the vitamin (or if a person is otherwise deficient in vitamin D, as is a large part of the population).

Antioxidants can help lower disease-causing free radicals (oxidants) in the brain and elsewhere in the body. This can prevent or stop cell damage caused by chemically unstable oxidants. These are waste products from normal cell functions like metabolism (using food for energy) and from external toxins like pollution, tobacco smoke, and alcohol. Oxidation in cells alters the chemical structure and a cell's function. Incidentally, once a person has significant dementia or Alzheimer's disease, it may be too late for antioxidants to help because these patients metabolize oxygen differently.

The studies on the benefits of antioxidant supplements are conflicted, so discuss these with a medical doctor. Here are a few to consider: fish oil (enteric coated), NAC (N-acetylcysteine), ALA (alpha lipoic acid), and vitamins C, E, D_3, and B complex.

Vitamin B_6 and B_{12} supplements might help in neurogenesis/ nerve cell regeneration. B_9 is a memory neurotransmitter.

Foods such as pomegranates, mangoes, blueberries, cherries, red grapes, whey protein, green tea, curry, and turmeric are high in antioxidants.

Drink Alcohol in Moderation and Stay Smoke-Free

Every time you reach for an addictive drug, stop and picture yourself nonfunctioning in a nursing home. It's not worth doing things that damage your brain. Tobacco and alcohol affect the body's ability to deliver oxygen and nutrients to the brain. They speed up the natural aging process and contribute to the formation of brain cell plaques that lead to dementia. Nicotine may temporarily increase neurocognitive functioning, attention, and working memory, but an addiction to nicotine can kill.

Alcohol is one of the most common drugs of abuse. A dependency can decrease life span by fifteen years and has been linked to health problems including almost all types of cognitive decline and dementia. Over time, it will lower brain volume and cause significant physical, psychological, and social consequences.

Some studies suggest that one drink a day for women and two drinks for men may reduce the risk of heart disease and dementia in older adults. I don't recommend taking up drinking alcoholic beverages, but low-dose consumption of certain types may be beneficial.

Get Health Checkups

Regular medical checkups from a family physician or internist are especially important for people over age fifty. If problems can be identified and treated in the early stages, they have a better chance of being stopped or cured. Make a note to discuss any memory concerns at your next health-care appointment.

Have the doctor review all your prescription medications and over-the-counter drugs. Older people metabolize medications at a slower rate and can reach toxic levels easier than younger adults. This combined with side effects and drug interactions can cause changes in mood, confusion, and memory loss.

Socialize

We all have a core need to be loved and accepted; support is one of the single most important psychological needs. Remind yourself every day that *relationships are more important than projects*. This truth may disrupt some of your routines or thought patterns, but it's for the good.

It has been said that a burden shared is only half a burden. We all need people to talk to. Spending time with family and friends engages areas of the brain that process attention, memory, and cognitive tasks. Make an effort to reach out to someone you know who may be lonely; it'll be good for both of you. And don't overlook your sibling relationships. Those natural bonds may need to be revived and nurtured.

Give Your Mind Results-Driven Workouts

In time, failing to challenge your brain can result in cerebral atrophy, or shrinking of the brain. Mental workouts increase the number of connections between nerve cells, which provides a range of ways for cells to communicate with each other and increases the speed with which they do it. Brain cell connections help you stay focused, anticipate and respond appropriately, recall memories, and process new information.

Stimulate your mind every day! This is doable even if you're a little unmotivated: read, play online brain games, do puzzles, practice new skills, play word games, learn something new, engage in hobbies, test your recall, do math in your head, draw things (like maps) from memory, practice hand-eye coordination, and listen to music. Try using your opposite hand for routine chores such as brushing your teeth, buttoning a shirt, tying shoelaces, or writing your name. This strengthens neural connections and even grows new ones. It's like physical exercise that improves body functions and develops muscles.

Having a stimulating environment is also helpful. Pet birds in cages need a variety of challenging and diverse environments for healthy physical and mental stimulation. The same is true for people. Take short car trips or different routes around town for a change of scenery. Meet friends at different places for coffee and conversation. Go to movies and local sporting events and take walks in different parks. Whatever activity you choose, venture out of your comfort zone.

Famous People in History

Are the following facts about these famous people in history correct? Even one incorrect entry renders a false answer for the entire chart.

		True (correct)	False (incorrect)
	Adam and Eve, first man and woman	_____	_____
470–399 BC	Socrates, a classical Greek philosopher	_____	_____
460–370 BC	Hippocrates, a Greek physician	_____	_____
428–348 BC	Plato, student of Socrates and teacher of Aristotle	_____	_____
384–322 BC	Aristotle taught Alexander the Great	_____	_____
69–30 BC	Cleopatra, the last active pharaoh of Ptolemaic Egypt	_____	_____
5 BC–AD 33	Jesus Christ, the central figure of Christianity	_____	_____
1492	Christopher Columbus discovered America	_____	_____

		True (correct)	False (incorrect)
1776	Thomas Jefferson and the Declaration of Independence	_____	_____
1905	Einstein and E=MC²	_____	_____
1969	man walked on the moon—Apollo 11	_____	_____
1981–89	Ronald Reagan served as president of the United States	_____	_____
2009	Barack Obama inaugurated as president of the United States	_____	_____

Math Concepts

Knowing a math concept means you know the workings behind the answer. Because you know why things work, you can figure out the answers and formulas yourself. This allows you to think and process abstractly.

Are the following mathematical concepts defined correctly? Even one inaccuracy renders the entire statement incorrect/false.

		True	False
1. algebra	a mathematical system that solves arithmetic problems through the use of letters to stand for numbers	_____	_____
2. geometry	a mathematical system involving relationships of points, lines, planes, and solids	_____	_____
3. trigonometry	angles of triangles	_____	_____
4. abscissa	x is the horizontal distance of a point from a vertical scale	_____	_____
5. ordinate	y is the vertical distance of a point from a horizontal scale	_____	_____
6. integers	whole numbers both positive and negative	_____	_____

		True	False
7. prime number	divisible only by 1 and the number itself	____	____
8. right angle	an angle of 90 degrees	____	____
9. distance	= rate x time; d = rt	____	____
10. hypotenuse	the longest side of a right triangle; the side opposite the 90 degree angle	____	____
11. Pi (Π)	the ratio between the circumference of a circle and its diameter; Π = 3.1416; Π = c/d = circumference/diameter	____	____

Biology Definitions

Biology is the study of life and living organisms (origins, growth, reproduction, structure, and behavior), from one-celled creatures to the most complex living organism of all, the human being. It includes the study of genes and cells that give living things their special characteristics.

Are all the following biology definitions and concepts correct?

		True	False
1. biology	the study of living organisms	____	____
2. acids	chemical compounds that release hydrogen ions in solution	____	____
3. bases	chemical compounds that accept hydrogen ions in solution	____	____
4. nucleic acids	large molecules that contain the genetic code for that organism	____	____
5. cytoplasma	semiliquid substance that contains organelles	____	____
6. organelles	microscopic bodies within the cytoplasm that perform distinct functions	____	____
7. ribosomes	organelle bodies bound to the endoplasmic reticulum that are the sites of protein synthesis	____	____

		True	False
8. Golgi	an organelle that is the site of protein and apparatus lipid processing	_____	_____
9. enzymes	proteins that catalyze chemical reactions within cells	_____	_____
10. mitochondria	the organelle that is the site of energy production within cells	_____	_____
11. nucleus	the organelle that contains the genetic material DNA	_____	_____
12. diffusion	the movement of molecules from a region of higher concentration to one of lower concentration	_____	_____
13. osmosis	diffusion involving only water molecules and often across a semipermeable membrane	_____	_____
14. adenosine	the chemical that provides the energy in cells' triphosphate (ATP)	_____	_____
15. photosynthesis	the process in plants of utilizing energy to synthesize carbohydrates	_____	_____
16. Krebs cycle	the subdivision of cellular respiration in which pyruvic acid is broken down and the resulting energy is used to form high-energy compounds	_____	_____

		True	False
17. mitosis	a type of cell division occurring in phases that results in two daughter cells each with the same number and kind of chromosomes as the parent cell; the process by which cells reproduce	___	___
18. meiosis	a type of cell division by which the chromosome number is halved during gamete formation; the process by which sperm cells and egg cells are produced	___	___
19. genome	the set of all genes that specify an organism's traits	___	___
20. genotype	the gene composition of a living organism	___	___
21. phenotype	the expression of the genes of a living organism	___	___
22. taxonomy	the science of classification of organisms	___	___
23. invertebrates	animals with no backbones, such as sponges, jellyfish, tapeworms, roundworms, earthworms, snails, squids, oysters, octopuses, spiders, ticks, lobsters, insects, sea urchins, and some reptiles	___	___
24. vertebrates	animals with backbones, such as fish, amphibians, some reptiles, birds, and mammals	___	___

Know Your Words 4

Learn these definitions for seven words.

Even if you already know some of the following words, practice using them more often in conversations.

Review new words over a period of weeks to help store them in your permanent memory.

chagrin: humiliation
chimera: an illusion
churl: a rude person
circa: about
circumspect: cautious
clandestine: secretive
cobble: to bind

Boost Your "Mental Homework" Time

If you're finding it more and more difficult to remember things or you want to boost your memory power, consider the following tips and work them into your routines.

Determine your *best biological time of day*. Are you sharper in the early morning or late at night? Use these personal peak times for reading, paperwork, and mind games.

Use your time wisely. Find *spare moments* each day for mental exercise. I studied countless hours but in bits of time by carrying around summary cards and pages of my notes— a moment here and a moment there. You'll find more of these moments if you watch for them and simplify your routines and tasks. I used spare moments to write about fifty books.

For big learning projects, break them down into *small parts*. Notice how books are divided into chapters. If you read one chapter each day, you'll soon complete the whole book.

Have *organized places* to read and study, with a comfortable chair and good lighting. Declutter these "thinking" areas.

Take *short breaks* every twenty to thirty minutes. Walk around, stretch, get something to drink, or step outside for some fresh air. This helps you stay alert.

Keep *clocks and calendars* in the rooms where you spend the most time.

Keep a *smartphone or notebook* handy to keep track of names, phone numbers, appointments, lists, errands, addresses and directions, and so on.

It's easy to lose track of time. Set *alarms* for important things you need to do. Put *sticky notes* around the house as reminders to do important things you might forget.

If you want to remember something, *say it aloud*—several times. I often do this when I'm driving alone in the car.

Before going to bed, decide on the three *most important tasks* for the next day and write them down. Doing so will get each new day off to a good start.

Make mental homework a *priority*.

Practice Memory Techniques

There are many memory techniques—mnemonics are systems for improving and assisting the memory. They help us remember information.

The most common types are music (lyrics and tunes), name (first letter in each word for a list of items), expression/word (first letter of each item in a list to form a phrase or word), model (pie charts, sequence or pyramid models), ode (in the form of a poem or rhyme), note organization (note cards, outlines, questions and answers), image (pictures that promote recall of information), connection (information connected to something already known), and spelling (splitting words into smaller words or letter combinations).[14]

You probably already use some of these techniques without even realizing it. Try as many as you can, and choose the ones that work best for you.

Visualization with exaggeration and linking helps vocabulary and improves short-term memory. Examples:

Visualize interesting *synonyms* for the word *big*: Imagine you are strolling down the beach when you see an enormous ship. Your mind sees a myriad of (many) people boarding the ship. The boat is capacious (roomy). The ship is headed to a megalopolis (you have a friend named Meg who lives in the city, so you can link to megalopolis).

Visualize and link a *list of items*: You need to buy milk, coconuts, bananas, and bread. Visualize a monkey swinging through the trees (coconut and banana trees). The coconut has milk in it, and you know a great banana bread recipe. Now you've linked in your mind all of the objects you need to buy.

Use *exaggerations* or funny sentences for recall. Example:

To remember a person by the name of Longman, visualize a man who is very long or tall; exaggerate it in your mind.

Use *associations* by connecting new information with old (common) information. Examples:

The music treble clef (E, G, B, D, F) is recalled with, "Every Good Boy Does Fine."
In geography, Italy is easily remembered by many because it is shaped like a boot.
When using a screwdriver or faucet, think of "lefty loosey, righty tighty."

Acronyms are formed from the initial letters of other words and pronounced as a word. Example:

In medical school I learned the symptoms of dementia with "IMAJO" (meaning impairment in Intellect, Memory, Affect, Judgment, and Orientation).

Pictures on Coins and Bills

The US Treasury announced in 2016 the twenty-dollar bill will feature Harriet Tubman on the front, with Andrew Jackson and an image of the White House on the back. The new five-dollar and ten-dollar bills will feature women and civil rights leaders on the back. The circulation date has yet to be released.

Whose pictures are on US coins and bills? Are all of the following correct?

Coin or Bill	Picture	True	False
1. one cent/penny	Lincoln	_____	_____
2. five cents/nickel	Jefferson	_____	_____
3. ten cents/dime	Roosevelt	_____	_____
4. twenty-five cents/quarter	Washington	_____	_____
5. one-dollar bill	Washington	_____	_____
6. five-dollar bill	Lincoln	_____	_____
7. ten-dollar bill	Hamilton	_____	_____
8. twenty-dollar bill	Jackson	_____	_____
9. fifty-dollar bill	Reagan	_____	_____
10. one-hundred-dollar bill	Franklin	_____	_____

Functions of the Mind

Psychology is the study of how the human mind functions, including the attitude, behavior, thinking, and reasoning of who we are. Naturally, it includes how to improve memory.

Are the following statements correct (true) or incorrect (false)?

	True	False
1. Memory is stored in vocabulary, concepts (knowledge), and visualization. A photographic memory can be developed to a degree through practice.	____	____
2. Neuroplasticity refers to the lifelong capacity of the brain to change and rewire itself in response to the stimulation of learning and experience.	____	____
3. The subconscious mind is like a memory bank with a virtually unlimited capacity. It permanently stores everything that ever happens to you.	____	____
4. Thinking involves the mediation of ideas or data when we form concepts and engage in problem-solving, reasoning, and decision-making.	____	____
5. The mind is a set of cognitive faculties including consciousness, perception, thinking, judgment, and memory.	____	____

	True	False
6. Cognition includes perception, attention, working memory, long-term memory, producing and understanding language, learning, reasoning, problem-solving, and decision-making.	___	___
7. Social psychology studies how humans think about and relate to each other.	___	___
8. Personality deals with patterns of behavior, thought, and emotion in individuals.	___	___
9. Developmental psychology seeks to understand how people come to perceive, understand, and act and how these processes change as they age.	___	___
10. Educational psychology studies how we learn in educational settings, the effectiveness of educational interventions, and the psychology of teaching.	___	___

Know Your English

Learning reading, spelling, literature, and composition develops our comprehension and use of the written and oral language.

Are the following concepts defined correctly?[15]

		True	False
1. noun	a part of speech that names a person, place, or thing	____	____
2. verb	a part of speech that indicates an action	____	____
3. pronoun	a word that replaces a noun	____	____
4. tense	a form taken by a verb to indicate the time of action, such as present, past, future, present perfect, past perfect, and future perfect	____	____
5. indicative mood	a verb form that makes a statement	____	____
6. imperative mood	a verb form that expresses a command	____	____
7. adjective	a part of speech that modifies a verb, an adjective, or an adverb	____	____
8. adverb	a part of speech that modifies a noun	____	____

		True	False
9. preposition	a part of speech that connects, such as *at, through, by, on, across, for, like, with,* and *to*	____	____
10. conjunction	a joining word that links parts of sentences, such as *and* or *but*	____	____

There's Something Special about These Times

It's an unusually fruitful era when it comes to words. You're lucky if you still have teenagers in your life because keeping up with their vocabulary can make you "cool" and exercise your brain at the same time. The trending words, slang, and emojis are continually morphing. Learning this viral language gives your brain a workout.

Many words and phrases have been shortened to abbreviations and acronyms. Tumblr, YouTube, and Twitter are leading this slang game. Try using some of the following when you text your kids or grandkids. It will blow their minds.

KMU—keep me updated

IMU—I miss you

QAP—quick as possible

GLWT—good luck with that

HW—homework

NON—now or never

HYB—how you been?

YDU—you don't understand

IGHT—alright, okay

IDK—I don't know

WUW—what you want?

N/C—not cool

It's also challenging to understand how words that have real meanings aren't always used properly anymore.

Salty—Bitter, upset. Example: "She's really salty she couldn't get the day off yesterday."

Clutch—This term means "cool" or "job well done." Example: "Your kitchen remodel is so clutch."

Fire—Superhot and trendy. Example: "Where did you get those comfy looking shoes? They're fire."

Gucci—Derived from the name of the upscale fashion retailer, this term means "really cool." Example: "Your new stand-up desk? That's Gucci."

Mental Exercise with Words

It's a Fact: We think in words. We communicate in words. Memory is largely stored in words. Thoughts become words, and words become actions.

Some words are just plain fun to say. Read the following aloud and enjoy:

ballyhoo (sensational publicity)

cattywampus (in disarray)

collywobbles (bellyache)

flibbertigibbet (frivolous, flighty person)

gobbledygook (unclear, wordy jargon)

hootenanny (informal folk performance)

itty-bitty (very small)

lollygag (waste time in aimless activity)

namby-pamby (weak, indecisive person)

piffle (nonsense)

snickersnee (long knife)

tintinnabulation (ringing sound of bells)

williwaw (violent gust of cold wind)

zedonk (offspring of a zebra and donkey)

Learn Words
for Your Brain's Sake

To stimulate your memory, I suggest learning or reviewing at least a few new words each day. Every word learned triggers another memory because words and definitions are connected to others. This mental exercise increases brainpower.

How to learn new words:

Read. The more pleasure reading you do, the better. Most new words are learned from seeing them in a book or magazine. The more words you're exposed to, the better vocabulary you'll have. Reading aloud gives your mental exercise an extra boost.

Learn new words in phrases or in a sentence so you'll remember the context.

Pay attention to how words are used. The context of a new word in a sentence or story is often enough to guess the meaning. You'll pick up vocabulary without even realizing it.

Write down words and definitions, then practice using them in sentences. The more you say them, the better you'll remember.

Make up word associations and connections with pictures or other words.

Play with words. Play Scrabble and Boggle and do crossword puzzles. Many word games are available online and in leisure workbooks.

Get in the habit of looking up the definitions of words you don't know.

Repeat. Research shows that it takes ten to twenty uses or memory repetitions to make a word part of your vocabulary.[16] Seeing and using the word again and again helps you retain it.

Homographs

Words that are often heard together (such as salt and pepper) or words that share some of their meaning (such as nurse and doctor) are connected or associated in the brain. The following brainteaser will stimulate the connections or associations between words in your brain. You will see pairs of words; the goal is to find a third word that is connected or associated with both of these two words. For example, consider the pair *piano* and *lock*. The answer is *key*. There are *keys* on a piano and you use a *key* to lock doors. *Key* is called a homograph, a word that has more than one meaning but is always spelled the same.

Are you ready to stimulate connections in your brain? What is the homograph for each pair?[17]

1. ship/card =
2. tree/car =
3. school/eye =
4. pillow/court =
5. river/money =
6. bed/paper =
7. army/water =
8. tennis/noise =
9. Egyptian/mother =
10. smoker/plumber =

The Magic of Prefixes, Suffixes, and Roots

Knowing common prefixes, suffixes, and root words and how to use them can unlock the meaning of thousands of words. Each prefix might hold the key to one hundred words.

For example, *mal* means "bad." Knowing this, you can guess the meaning of malabsorption, maladapted, maladjusted, maladministration, maladroit, malady, malaise, malapropos, malcontent, malediction, malefactor, malfeasance, malformation, malfunction, malignancy, malinger, malnourished, malpractice, and maltreatment.[18]

Idioms

Idioms are expressions that make no sense if translated literally. Can you interpret the following idioms and use each one in a sentence?

flash in the pan

on the warpath

cold feet

sitting duck

eat crow

wet blanket

green thumb

tip of the iceberg

hold water

throw the book at someone

know the ropes

split hairs

lion's share

shot in the dark

play possum

run of the mill

tongue-in-cheek

glad-hander

wet behind the ears

under the wire

What Can Make You Smarter and More Successful?

Reading. It's better for your brain than playing on your smartphone while you kill time at airports or relax at home. Personal electronics keep your brain flitting and multitasking throughout the day. But when you read a book, your attention stays focused and steady. Put your smartphone down and read for fifteen to twenty minutes before you go to work or start your day. Your stress level will decrease and your concentration will increase.

Reading can also help you be more successful in anything you do because being well-read, articulate, and knowledgeable in a variety of topics is important in almost every occupation.

Reading

- keeps the memory and learning capacity sharp
- expands vocabulary and improves spelling and communication skills
- develops analytical skills, concentration, and creativity
- encourages positive thinking, empathy, and motivation and boosts self-confidence
- reduces stress and the risk of dementia and Alzheimer's disease
- increases blood flow and stimulates different areas of the brain

It's interesting that the level of mental exercise varies with different types of reading. For instance, reading a novel for literary study exercises more complex cognitive functions than pleasure reading. The more difficult the reading, the greater the benefits.

Reading changes the brain. Not everyone is a good reader, but poor readers can be trained, which changes and boosts their brain structure. Reading is a complex process involving different centers of the brain working together to increase the connectivity between various neural circuits. For example, the cerebrum interprets vision and hearing, speech, emotions, learning, and fine movement. Language, memory, problem-solving, judgment, and reasoning are managed in the frontal lobes. The left temporal cortex is associated with receptivity for language. And the angular and supramarginal gyrus link these parts of the brain together to execute reading.

Get something good to read. There are enough reading categories to interest everyone throughout their lifetime: fiction, nonfiction, biographies, self-help, hobbies, travel, science fiction, history, youth, resources, guides, mysteries, classical literature, satires, anthologies, religion, and more. Books entertain and help us understand different cultures and societies, and they relate history and concepts to today's world.

Get a free library card from your local library or download some ebooks. It may take a week or so to get used to an e-reader, but your brain will adapt. It's fast, easy, inexpensive, and portable. Audiobooks are another good option for car trips and long commutes. When listening to reading or reading aloud, different brain circuits are used than when you read silently to yourself.

One more thing: consider turning off the TV sometimes. Reading is more neurologically demanding. Most television programming doesn't stimulate the brain; that's why it's so relaxing. The brain just processes images and speech, and the visual imagery is automatic. At least choose to watch more educational programs or ones with complex plotlines and characters, so you can engage your brain.

Building Your Cognitive Reserve

Because cognitive function peaks in the early thirties, do all you can do to keep your brain fit so you can keep living a vital life for the next four to five decades. Cognition is more than just memorization. It is insight, perception, discernment, comprehension, and learning; it is the process of acquiring knowledge and understanding.

People who have cognitive reserves can be more resistant to age-related brain changes or Alzheimer's disease. They are also less likely to show early signs of dementia, such as short-term memory loss and difficulty multitasking.

At some point in the future, you or a family member may be evaluated by a medical professional for possible cognitive impairment. Anyone with memory concerns needs an initial screening evaluation. You may be unaware that all Medicare beneficiaries can be screened as part of the annual wellness visit. This was initiated in 2011 as part of the Affordable Care Act. It includes a patient history, clinician observations, and concerns expressed by the patient or family.[19] Simple assessment tools can detect possible dementia and determine if additional evaluations are needed. These screening tests may include the General Practitioner Assessment of Cognition exam, the "MiniCog" screening for Cognitive Impairment in Older Adults, a Memory Impairment Screen, an Informant Interview to Differentiate Aging and Dementia, or a Short Informant Questionnaire of Cognitive Decline in the Elderly.[20] These tools include most of the symptoms listed in the self-assessment in chapter 1 or in the mental exercises below.

Consider working with a partner and adding these mental exercises to your routine:

- *Verbal memory*—Give three (to ten) words to remember and ask to repeat now and again later.
- *Verbal fluency*—Give sixty seconds to name as many words as possible in a word category (e.g., foods, pets, recreation). Next, give sixty seconds to name as many words as possible that begin with a given letter.
- *Working memory*—Give random numbers of increasing size and ask to repeat the numbers from highest to lowest.
- *Motor speed*—Place one hundred small tokens (one at a time) into a container for sixty seconds as quickly as possible.
- *Information*—Tell something that happened in the news in the last week, with as many details as possible.
- *Emotional distractibility and memory*—Give twenty words: ten objects (e.g., ball, cracker) and ten with emotional value (e.g., romance, cancer). Ask to recall all the words, then recall the two lists separately.

These assessments may be given in a clinical setting:

- *Reasoning and problem-solving*—Look at two pictures simultaneously; each picture shows three different colored balls arranged differently on three pegs. Determine the fewest number of times the balls in one picture would need to be moved to make the arrangement identical to the opposing picture.
- *Attention and processing speed*—Various timed matching and sorting exercises.

Give Your Brain a Change of Pace

Weekends are fun because of the change of pace. So are vacations and holidays. But to go a step further, it helps your mind when you mix up routines with different activities. Try some new things and break up your routines.

Choose brain-building activities that are reasonably complex, varied, new, and challenging and do them frequently. For instance, try some online brain fitness apps. They probably won't make you smarter or happier, but they may help you perform certain tasks better. You won't notice any drastic transformation, but it's worth a try. Any cognitively demanding tasks are a good change of pace for your brain. Here are some ideas:

- Learn some conversational words in a foreign language.
- Switch around your morning activities and try to do things with the opposite hand.
- Trade seats around the dinner table; it changes conversations and the view of the room.
- Open the car windows and notice the sounds and smells on your route.
- Stay informed about what's going on in the world.
- Read books and newspapers; join a book club.

- Tutor reading or other areas of interest to the young or elderly or to people who use English as their second language.
- Volunteer (social connections are good for your brain).
- Do your own math; resist using a calculator.
- Turn tabletop pictures, clocks, or a calendar upside down.
- At the grocery store, stop and look at the shelves, top to bottom. If there's something you've never seen before, read the ingredients and think about it. You don't have to buy it to benefit.
- Visit cultural sites when you travel.
- Visit area museums and historic sites in the county where you live.
- Shop at new grocery stores and cook new recipes.
- Try new hobbies.
- Play "thinking" games such as Scrabble, cards, checkers, or chess.

PART 3

STRESS
AND
YOUR BRAIN

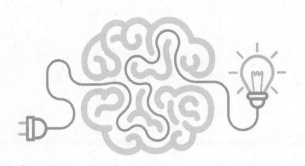

Self-Assessment: Stress-Level Symptoms

Stress produces a variety of physical, psychological, mental, and behavioral symptoms. It can also trigger an illness or aggravate existing health problems.

It matters how you personally handle it. The best way is to keep track of all your symptoms. By rating the following common signs of chronic stress, you may be able to determine if it's an acceptable, manageable factor in your lifestyle or if it has become detrimental to your overall health.

The list below is not comprehensive and is not a standardized medical evaluation. It simply provides an overview of possible symptoms that may help you become more aware of your emotional and physical well-being. It's a starting point for making new choices for improving your health.

Please rate each of the symptoms on a scale of 0 to 10. This will help you assess your stress intensity levels so you can work on eliminating stressors or increasing your tolerance level.

0 = none

1, 2, or 3 = mild/minor/noticeable—annoying but doesn't interfere with daily activities

4, 5, or 6 = moderate/moderately strong—interferes with daily activities

7, 8, or 9 = disabling/intense—unable to perform daily activities

10 = severe

Emotional Symptoms

depression, feeling sad, crying spells _____
frequent mood swings _____
worried, upset _____
anxious, nervous, restless _____
agitation, frustration, feeling overwhelmed _____
anger, outbursts, irritability, hostility, annoyance _____
low motivation, few interests _____
trouble paying attention, distractible, forgetful _____
tense, difficulty relaxing _____
low self-esteem, lonely _____
fearful, defensive, suspicious _____
upsetting dreams _____
burnout, emotional exhaustion _____
other _____

Cognitive Symptoms

confusion, poor judgment, difficulty making decisions _____
forgetful, disorganized _____
unable to focus or concentrate, racing thoughts _____
difficulty communicating _____
stuttering, stammering, can't think of words _____
trouble learning new information _____
irrational worrying _____
pessimistic, focusing on negatives _____
other _____

Behavioral Symptoms

obsessive compulsions or repetitive actions _____

trouble functioning at work, at home, or socially _____

avoiding others, social withdrawal _____

procrastination, avoiding responsibilities _____

increased use of alcohol, drugs, or cigarettes _____

nervous habits: fidgeting, nail-biting, pacing _____

increased addictions such as shopping, gambling _____

more minor accidents, clumsy _____

lies or excuses to cover up actions _____

inefficient, unproductive _____

excessive or inappropriate use of over-the-counter
    drugs _____

poor grooming and hygiene, disinterest in appearance _____

rapid or mumbled speech _____

other _____

Physical Symptoms

insomnia, difficulty falling or staying asleep, changed sleeping
    habits, nightmares _____

jaw clenching, gritting or grinding teeth _____

faint, dizzy, light-headed _____

allergy episodes _____

muscle tension, aches, spasms, or pain _____

frequent headaches _____

heartburn, stomach pain, nausea, indigestion _____

constipation, diarrhea _____

frequent urination _____

fatigue, low energy, weakness _____

chest pain, rapid heartbeat _____

frequent colds and infections _____

loss of sexual desire and/or ability _____

dry mouth _____

panic attacks _____

shaking, trembling, twitching _____

shortness of breath, frequent sighing _____

ear ringing, popping, or buzzing _____

hot flashes, blushing, sweating _____

cold or sweaty hands, feet _____

rashes, itching, hives _____

excessive belching or flatulence _____

changes in appetite or weight _____

other _____

Managing Stress
in Your Peak Years

Some adult roles are changing because of a current trend that's impacting many families across America. Grown children are moving back home, and elderly parents are living longer and needing help. Even though families are dispersed across the country, most adults are getting involved in caring for multiple generations.

The following is more than an example; it's a warning that chronic stress is threatening the brain health of many adults in their peak years.

People in the traditional "sandwich generation" are in their thirties, forties, and more recently, their fifties. They're taking care of their children as well as meeting the needs of their aging parents who are living longer and needing supervised care.

Young adults ranging from ages of twenty-five to thirty-four are becoming known as the "boomerang generation." It's more common for them to live with their parents because of economic hardships. The "sandwiched" adults are now responsible for helping two generations, in addition to taking care of themselves, with daily routines, medical services, supervision, medications, finances, and the legal and emotional needs of their loved ones. This affects the caregivers' finances, personal time, careers, and mental health. They are succumbing to stress and burnout.

The "club sandwich generation" includes those in their fifties and sixties sandwiched between aging parents, adult children, and grandchildren, or those in their thirties and forties with young children, aging parents, and grandparents. The "open-faced genera-tion" is anyone else involved in elder care.[1]

All of these situations and relationships are different, so there are no right or wrong ways to manage chronic stress. But here are a few ideas that may help those caught in the multigenerational maze:

- Set boundaries for financial spending for both the grown children and the elderly parents and stay within the agreed-upon budgets.
- Communicate. Regularly gather all three generations to discuss tasks, schedules, and finances. Seek outside help for unmet needs.
- Mentor children over eighteen to prepare to live indepen-dently.
- Consider having aging parents move into your home. Three generations living together is becoming a more popular trend. It saves time and money. Caregivers can claim tax benefits and medical-care reductions, and de-duct the medical bills on tax returns. At least do the math.
- Take care of yourself. The needs of caregivers often get overlooked.

Do Less

Every now and then rest your brain. Relaxing can sharpen memory and improve creativity, productivity, and reaction time. These quick tips can decrease your stress and improve your brain function and are more therapeutic than you may think.

Say "no." Something's got to give. Trying to do everything for everybody all the time is a dangerous lifestyle that won't end well. Know your limits, and make sure the people around you are clear on them too. Don't attempt more than you can handle. It's okay to say no; it leaves more time and energy for the yeses. And you don't need to explain yourself or keep apologizing. It may even help those around you develop some independence and skills.

Take a catnap. Ten-minute naps can improve alertness for up to three hours. Anything longer may interfere with nighttime sleep and make you feel groggy.

Stop the daily grind. Stress can settle in your jaws. Teeth gritting and grinding cause mental exhaustion, facial pain, damaged teeth, and poor sleep quality. During the day, try putting the tip of your tongue between your teeth to relax jaw muscles when you feel stressed. Stop chewing gum because it keeps your jaw muscles used to clenching. At night, consider a mouth/bite guard (custom-made are best), avoid caffeine and alcohol, and relax your jaw muscles by holding a warm washcloth against your cheek in front of your earlobe.

Change the Activity

Walk it out. Brief, brisk walks can clear your head and relieve stress. Walking also increases blood circulation and gets more oxygen to the brain. Step outside or find a long hallway. It doesn't matter when or where, just move. It lifts your mood and, even better, grab someone to go with you. It'll make their day.

Do a five-second shake. Stress can tighten the muscles in your neck, shoulders, and back. While standing or sitting, look up, stretch your arms out to your sides, and shake your hands hard. Combine this with a smile and a few deep breaths.

Cheer up your brain. Our brains are interconnected with our emotions and facial expressions. When people are stressed, it shows in their faces. Laughing and smiling relieve some of that tension and may even improve some situations.

Stand tall. When people are stressed, they can neglect their posture, as if they're carrying the weight of the world on their shoulders. Over time, certain muscles tighten or shorten while others lengthen and become weak. Poor posture can result in long-term neck, shoulder, and back pain. Slumping also reduces blood and oxygen flow to the brain, restricts breathing, and tenses muscles. Straightening your spine has the opposite effect; it promotes circulation, increases oxygen levels in your blood, and helps lessen muscle tension, all of which relieve stress.

Let Your Mind Wander

Get lost. Take short mental breaks and let your mind wander. Get lost in your thoughts and daydream about things you want to see or do.

Look forward. Make plans for special activities in the coming months. It's hard to get away from a stressful job, needy kids, credit card bills, and long lists of projects, but looking forward to something fun like a movie marathon, lunch with friends, or a short road trip can give you a calming perspective. Short, spontaneous breaks are great too.

Change What You're Consuming

Eat right. Foods high in carbohydrates stimulate the release of serotonin, a feel-good brain chemical that helps induce calm. But there are good carbs and bad carbs. People trying to feel better may overeat bad (refined) carbs like potato chips, sugary drinks, and pastries. That's why they may gain weight when stressed.

Cut down caffeine. Caffeine affects people differently, partly because genetics influence our response to caffeine. Its effects are long lasting and can compound stress or the perception of stress. Caffeine is a mild stimulant to the central nervous system so if you take it habitually, your brain learns when the drug is coming and gets ready to react. Half the time drink caffeine, and the other half drink decaf. Coffee or tea could even be mixed half and half. Your brain will stop associating the drink with a caffeine response. Also switch up when and where you drink caffeine so your brain will stop associating caffeine with those times and places. Wean yourself slowly to avoid caffeine-withdrawal headaches. Over a few weeks, gradually increase the proportion of decaf drinks.

Avoid self-medication. Alcohol and over-the-counter drugs can add to your problems.

Get plenty of *sleep*, *exercise*, and *good nutrition*.

Get Perspective

Make two lists. Get a new perspective by looking at the big picture. Make a list of the stressors you might be able to change or avoid. Make another list of the things you can't change. Change what you can from the first list, such as avoiding heated topics or finding time for yourself. Stop stressing over things out of your control, such as changing your supervisor's management style or healing an elderly parent.

Choose a motto. Biochemicals flush through your body when the stress response turns on, and your brain goes into an alarm state. Decide on a short, positive statement that calms you, such as "I choose peace" or "I can handle this." Close your eyes and repeat your motto three times every time you feel stressed.

Change Your Location

Find comfort. There's something comforting about warmth and darkness. Rub the palms of your hands together fast until they feel warm. Then cup them over your closed eyes and breathe slowly. This common trick is so quick and easy that it can be done almost any time any place. Try it now.

Try the child pose. Muscles tighten over the course of the day, and when you're stressed, the process speeds up. Stretching loosens muscles and encourages deep breathing. The stress-relieving yoga "child pose" position can calm your mind and body. Find a comfortable place to kneel, sit back on your heels, then lean forward and put your forehead on the floor. Lay your arms by your legs with your palms up, then close your eyes. Ease into this position by relaxing your shoulders and neck. You'll feel a gentle stretch in your shoulders and down the length of your spine and arms. Hold this position for at least two to three minutes.

Take a mini-time-out. Count to five before you say or do something you might regret. Step away from the stressor for a moment, walk around the room, or put the caller on hold. Use your mini-time-out to take a few deep breaths, stretch, or recite your calming motto.

Relax to Help Your Memory

Breathe in deeply then exhale the stress. Shallow chest breathing can cause your heart to beat faster and your muscles to tense up, making feelings of stress even worse. Deep belly breathing oxygenates the blood, which helps you relax almost instantly. Inhale slowly through your nose, hold the breath for a few seconds, then exhale slowly and repeat.

Adjust your lifestyle to include more leisure time and healthy relationships. *Build your support system* of family, friends, neighbors, church members, and coworkers. Discuss your concerns with a trusted person. Talking relieves strain, puts things in perspective, and may lead to a plan of action.

Practice relaxation techniques such as progressive muscle relaxation, guided visual imagery, relaxed breathing, meditation, and prayer.

Change Your Thinking

Practice positive thinking such as, "Life is difficult, but not hopeless," "I'll start looking for options," or "Bad choices hurt, so I'll make better choices."

Challenge inaccurate thinking such as, "This situation will never get better," "This is all my fault," "I'll only be happy when . . . ," "No one cares," "I must be perfect," "There's no way out," or "The future is hopeless."

Try to avoid denial, isolation or withdrawal, blaming yourself or others, anger, rationalization, or becoming controlling or passive-aggressive.

Ask for help. There are many books and online resources available. Live, individualized counseling and medical assistance may be more helpful to some.

PART 4

ANXIETY
AND
YOUR BRAIN

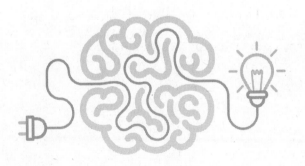

Change Your Diet

Stop consuming caffeine, or drastically reduce products that contain caffeine, such as coffee, tea, cola, energy drinks, and chocolate.

Consult a doctor or pharmacist before taking any over-the-counter medicines or herbal remedies. Many contain chemicals that can increase anxiety symptoms.

Avoid eating late at night.

Avoid skipping meals, as this lowers your metabolic rate and energy level.

Guard your diet. Excessive sugar, alcohol, coffee, tea, and soft drinks can rob your system of the nutrients and energy it needs to manage anxiety.

Change Your Activity

Regular aerobic exercise reduces the level of stress-related hormones in the body. Start a graduated exercise routine, and stick with it.

Get adequate sleep. Most people need an average of seven and one-half hours of sleep per night.

Use a repetitive phrase (or visualize a favorite retreat) to help you unwind. Decide on a phrase like "calm down." When feeling anxious, say it over and over, and soon the phrase will trigger the desired action. Time and conditioning are required to make this method dependable.

Change Your Perspective

Consider the odds. About 95 percent of worries never come true, and most of life's catastrophes we never see coming. Worry is useless.

Live one day at a time. Obsessive worriers live in the future; depressive worriers live in the past. The future is not here; the past is gone. Live in the present.

Consider the probability. If the worry just won't go away, then take action. Prepare for the worst, and then improve on it (though often, the worst will not happen).

When you're feeling overwhelmed by details, remember to *focus on the big picture.* It may help you prioritize the details that are demanding your attention.

Appreciate the good things in your life. It's difficult to experience the feelings of anxiety and gratitude at the same time.

Reach Out to Others

Share with a friend. A very true, old adage says, "A burden shared is only half a burden." Build a few close friendships, and share often. Talk through your problems to get a fresh perspective. A study on communication determined that the average busy person spends 80 percent of their day communicating. The breakdown was 45 percent listening, 30 percent talking, 16 percent writing, and 9 percent reading.[1]

Seek help if you regularly feel anxious with no apparent cause. The encouragement and counsel from a professional can help put you in touch with the core issues and develop a plan to deal with them.

Get a medical evaluation and follow-up care.

Get counseling for insights, behavior (stress reduction), and cognition support.

Spend more time in a positive environment with supportive people. Share laughter, forgiveness, and patience.

Get spiritual support. People who are ill often ask spiritual questions in seeking comfort, meaning, and hope. They can draw on their spiritual beliefs and experience as a source of strength. Meditation and prayer can help the mind relax and focus.

Use Your Time
to Reduce Anxiety

Use the time-limit technique. Limit "worry time" to a specific fifteen-minute period every morning and another fifteen-minute period in the evening. Refuse to worry nonstop because it wastes your time and saps your energy.

Listen to soothing music. Did you ever wonder why stores provide easy listening music? It helps people slow down, so they can relax and stay longer in the present situation.

Relax. When you feel tense, drop your shoulders and breathe deeply. Then tense your hands, feet, and facial muscles, hold it, then release.

Challenge Your Thinking

Get the facts. Worries often fade with facts. Perhaps the big picture has been missed. Facts will help.

Reduce anxiety through cognitive choices. Choices are powerful in directing your daily life. Anxiety's source is in the mind, and it must be controlled, challenged, and redirected. It may help to rank your worries. Using a scale of 1 to 5, with 1 being a minor hassle and 5 being a crisis, assign a number to your worries. Those in the 1 to 3 range aren't a big deal. Let them go.

Better beliefs are needed. Inaccurate beliefs can increase anxiety. You can help keep your anxiety under control if you challenge cognitive distortions:

- "I'm not perfect. I'll move toward growth and forgive myself when I fail."
- "This situation is not the end of the world. God has everything under control."
- "I'm focusing too much on the negative. Much has gone well in my life."
- "Just because I think something is true does not mean it is true."
- "The future is not hopeless. Good can come out of bad."
- "Life is difficult but not hopeless. I can fight back."
- "Choosing bad thoughts hurts, so I will choose healthy thoughts."

- "People care to different degrees, often depending on their maturity levels."
- "Options may be difficult to see, but options do exist. I'll start looking."
- "Two are better than one."

Change Your Surroundings

Emotions are often "light sensitive." *Bring more light* into your home and office by opening your curtains and turning on another light. Find a hue that calms you—certain bulbs or light sources have pinkish, yellowish, or bluish tints.

Make a Plan

Make a plan of action. When troubles come, plan options, list good and bad options, then list crazy options. Then choose a few options you can implement now.

The brain records personal fears, anxieties, and trials. Knowing *why you hurt* might direct you toward the solutions.

Take action. "Pray to God, but row to shore" (Russian proverb).

PART 5

MEMORY
AND
PURPOSE

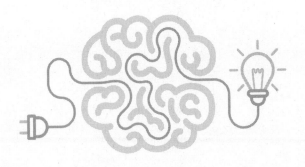

Revive Your Purpose

It's a Fact: Every time you recall a memory or have a new thought, a new connection is created in your brain.

As kids, we fantasized about buried treasure in the nearby woods or money lost in piles of leaves outside store entrances. We kept our eyes glued to the ground as we walked, scanning for good stuff. There was always potential for finding something special. We have that same potential in our lives today. We may have abilities that haven't been developed or goals that have been forgotten.

I often hear the buzz phrase, "Maximize your potential." It's fun to think about the potential our kids have. We dream big dreams for them, but we forget to keep our own visions in a growing mode.[1]

If I were to ask one hundred people what they ultimately hope to do or become, I would probably get one hundred different answers. Some may fantasize about being president of the United States, while others just want to make it through the day. Others' dreams may be to get off alcohol, heal a marriage, or survive cancer. These are all important visions because they are important to us and inspire positive action.

Leroy Eimes, who served the Navigators ministry for over fifty years, once asked a young man what he was going to do with his life now that he had finished school. The young man thought and thought. Finally he said, "I think I'll buy a Buick."

You may wonder if your goals are big or good enough. Maybe you are shortchanging yourself like this young man. Or maybe your goals need to stretch beyond your investment portfolio and the square footage of your home. Your vision will partially pivot around your relationships, and this is healthy. Your family, friends, colleagues, career, and hobbies not only keep you active but also probably support your life purpose.

In an online pop culture survey, some of the most common life goals young people listed are as follows:[2]

- being happy (content, satisfied)
- achieving intellectual growth (educational achievements)
- having financial freedom (wealth)
- having occupational success
- having close relationships
- having peace of mind
- caring for others, being charitable
- fulfilling personal morals (doing the right things, integrity)
- living Christian values
- pursuing passions
- having stability and safety
- being inspiring
- influencing others (leadership)
- being respected
- appreciating nature and beauty
- fulfilling social values (peace, justice, equality)

What Gets You
out of Bed Every Day?

What makes you tick? I believe people of all ages want a challenge, big or small, that sets them apart from everyone else. I want every person to convert their dreams into at least some degree of reality.

You made plans for yourself in your twenties, and you will do the same for your thirties and forties. If you're going to make a major change such as moving to another state or redirecting your career, it's likely you'll do it in one of those decades. Your work-life balance and contentment are probably at healthy levels, so it's the perfect time to assess your brain fitness along with your long-range goals. They work together. Your sense of accomplishment, mixed with hope and a can-do confidence, will help clarify your life purpose.

Every invention and masterpiece began with a dream, an intent that shows what's important to us. The brain tries hard to do what we want it to do. Having dreams and a life mission will keep us centered and growing.[3]

Keep Your Focus
on the Big Picture

Without purpose, nations fail and companies go bankrupt. Without purpose, churches wane and people drift. Without purpose, the brain slows. Perhaps you are unsure of or have temporarily lost sight of your life purpose. It's more than acquiring possessions, making money, or traveling the world. There is more than just doing things. It's living purposefully.

Your passions and related activities bring you fulfillment. The things you accomplish with your heart and talents are things that matter. It's your contribution over time that ultimately makes a difference.

Have you considered God's purpose for your life? In 1958 I found purpose, or rather, purpose found me. It was to have a ministry for Christ. I was twelve years old when Christ became my best friend. I never wanted to displease him then or since. I wanted to boost my brain, so I could be effective for him. This commitment always guided my major decisions. When I developed diabetes, I was fearful, but I committed to trust Christ and he blessed me.

Have you ever heard the old adage, "He can't see the forest through the trees"? The "trees" are all the details of a broad issue—in this case, keeping up with the demands of daily life. The "forest" is the big picture of your legacy. Someone who is so consumed with all the details may miss appreciating the results. I've seen this with homemakers who stew for months over a family holiday gathering but miss the joy of the event. I've seen it in workaholics who get burned out and lose their family and friends. They lose their balance and perspective of what really matters in their lives—relationships.

Sometimes it's hard to stay focused because of the barrage of demands on our time. Have you ever been so consumed by busyness that you missed the joy of a milestone? This often happens when people are building their careers, rearing children, or managing the seasons of marriage. When you're feeling overwhelmed by circumstances, stop and think of the big picture. Realize that many of the circumstances that can distract you are just temporary. This can help you prioritize details that consume your time. You'll realize that some projects or activities have nothing to do with supporting your priorities. These need to be phased out. Keep your energy aimed at the things that enhance your core interests. Stay on track.

If you look back and feel guilty that climbing the ladder of success was accomplished at the expense of your marriage, children, church, or health, forgive yourself and reset your focus. The same is true for memory care. If you've ignored regular brain exercise and now fear it's too late, it's not. It's never too late to take care of your mind.

You Can Lead a Purposeful Life

Contrary to common beliefs, statistics show that career retirement does not cause people to die earlier. According to data compiled by the Social Security Administration, a man reaching age 65 today can expect to live, on average, until age 84.3. A woman turning age 65 today can expect to live, on average, until age 86.6. And those are just averages. About one out of every four 65-year-olds today will live past age 90, and one out of ten will live past age 95.[4]

A growing number of Americans are living to age 100. The centenarian population has increased 65.8 percent in the past thirty years.[5] The bottom line is that most people will have over twenty years to enjoy retirement. This is precious time that can be used to make a difference.

Your circumstances and even some goals will change through each life stage, and this is normal. But will your core passions remain the same? Have they been a steady guide through all the years? We all struggle with this.

What do you want from life? What do you excel at? What do you want to accomplish? What do you care about the most? How do you want to be remembered after you die? Anyone over age twenty (which probably includes most readers of this book) needs to consider these questions and think about the following advice:

Focus on what consistently feels important to you. Choose activities that support your goals.

Look for the needs of others and work to make their lives better any way you can.

Be aware of your feelings but *focus on your behavior.* "You don't do what you do because you feel the way you feel— you feel the way you feel because you do what you do." You may need to read that a few times to fully grasp the concept and apply it to your experiences.[6]

Brainstorm about opportunities and act on the ones that boost your mission.

Be realistic and stay flexible. There are many ways to reach most goals.

Keep a balanced lifestyle physically, mentally, emotionally, and spiritually.

Socialize with others often (attend worship services, participate in activities, and nurture close family and friend relationships).

Stay active mentally.

Describe Yourself

Write words or phrases below that describe your unique qualities and choices.

1. Special characteristics:

2. Special skills and interests:

3. Key relationships:

4. Top priorities (most valued):

5. Major goals that are aligned with your values:

Now underline the words above that bring you the most joy and fulfillment. Use these words to draft your strategy for living purposefully.

You Can Preserve Your Mind

It's a Fact: The brain accounts for about 20 percent of energy needs, and uses 20 percent of the oxygen and blood circulating in our bodies.[7]

We spend a lot of time thinking about our heart and skin health because they're critical to our well-being and our looks. But how often do we think about caring for our most important organ, the brain?

Turn on the TV, scan magazines, and surf the internet, and you'll see a barrage of advertisements about how a person can look, feel, and stay young. Bald men can grow hair, and there is a miracle cream for every need. People think, "If I just do those exercises or take those pills . . ." The media has gone overboard to keep youthfulness alive. I wish they would give the same attention to promoting brain fitness for people of all ages. But thanks to the widespread use of the internet, many brain health resources are now accessible to almost every household in America. But this leads us to another issue.

Reboot Your Self-Help Commitment

There's a lot of evidence that what we do for our brains now can have a big impact on how they function in the years to come. Some of the risks for brain decline can't be controlled, such as a family history of mental illness. But there are many positive factors that we *can* control and that make a significant difference: being married, having at least two close friends, living in or regularly visiting a rural area, not smoking, routinely exercising, sleeping six to eight hours a night, being normal weight, eating fruits and vegetables, and not eating many fatty or sweet foods.[8]

But no matter how proactive we are, we can't keep our brains from changing with age and experiencing bouts of forgetfulness, absentmindedness, or mental fog.

"Umm . . . where did I park the car?"

"That lady looks familiar. . . . What's her name?"

Losing some mental clarity over time is normal. The most common causes are aging, chronic illness, chemical imbalances, medication side effects, substance abuse, medical conditions, nutritional deficiencies, lack of sleep, lack of mental and physical activity, and others. But even with all these risks stacked against us, there are just as many things we can do to counteract them. You're probably already aware of the best-known tips for memory care and even the science behind them. Some are simply common sense while others require knowledge, judgment, and choice. But actually incorporating them into your daily lifestyle is easier said than done. Procrastination and apathy can set in quickly.

It may help to have an accountability partner like a family member or friend to keep you motivated. Trust me, the short- and especially the long-term benefits are worth the effort.

Start now. Sometimes later becomes never.

Keep Feeding Your Brain

We eat three times a day to feed our bodies, so shouldn't we regularly feed information to our brains? This needs to be an ongoing process, not just random encounters. It's not enough to read something once and hope it sticks. This "feeding" can be fun because there is always something new to learn in your areas of interest. Read special-interest magazines and books. Surf favorite topics on the internet. The average person browses through about one hundred internet domains each month, according to a Nielsen estimate in 2013. But that's just a small start. There are about one billion sites on the internet, which provide a lot of food for thought.[9]

Trying to summarize the different types of knowledge is difficult because there's no master list. There are many opinions on knowledge categories, but for my purpose, I'll use these three: personal, procedural, and propositional.

> *Personal knowledge* is by acquaintance, the kind we have when we say things like "I know my spouse."
>
> *Procedural knowledge* is how to do something such as juggle or drive. It's having the knowledge to perform skills.
>
> *Propositional knowledge* is having facts. When we say things such as "I know that the three angles of a triangle add up to 180 degrees" or "I know you ate my pickle," we have propositional knowledge.

It's the propositional knowledge—the facts—that can build our intellect and improve our memory. Try to put a plan like the following into action:

- Make a list of your special interests and decide where you'll find new information about them. For instance, do you want to know more about crafting gifts, car repair, medical conditions, fitness, travel, entertainment, or fishing?
- Learn about and keep reviewing the new information in these areas to revitalize your brain circuits.
- Also study and review broad knowledge topics such as cultural literacy. The one hundred general knowledge facts in the Memory Boosters section (starting on p. 23) are designed to stimulate your brain. Once you find all the right answers, review them over and over.
- Keep learning new words and their meanings.
- Push your brain to reason better and to improve rapid processing of information. There are online exercises and memory games for that too.

Your job is to keep feeding knowledge to your brain. The goal is to keep the neurotransmitters, synaptic connections, and nerve impulses along the pathways of brain circuits, chemicals, and neurons all working together in a constant, smooth, organized process. Balance and harmony of the parts that store and process your memory are the goal.

To put it a simpler way, for neurons to become active, they must receive stimuli. Each neuron has many dendrites that receive electrical messages, and the dendritic fields can be increased through *personal education*. Keep your dendrites fired up!

Finish Well!

It's a Fact: You know what is good for your brain. Make wise choices today so you can feel better, think better, and live better tomorrow. The good thing about your brain is that the more you use it, the better it gets.

In April 2016, Patti Davis Reagan, author, actress, and daughter of President Ronald Reagan and Nancy Reagan, wrote the following testimony about her father's battle with Alzheimer's disease:

Alzheimer's doesn't care if you are President of the United States or a dockworker. It steals what is most precious to a human being—memories, connections, the familiar landmarks of a lifetime that we all come to rely on to hold our place secure in this world and keep us linked to those we have come to know and love. I watched as fear invaded my father's eyes—this man who was never afraid of anything. I heard his voice tremble as he stood in the living room and said, "I don't know where I am." I watched helplessly as he reached for memories, for words, that were suddenly out of reach and moving farther away. For ten long years he drifted—past the memories that marked his life, past all that was familiar . . . and mercifully, finally past the fear.

Alzheimer's is the ultimate pirate, pillaging a person's life and leaving an empty landscape behind. It sweeps up entire families, forcing everyone to claw their way through overwhelming grief, confusion, helplessness, and anger. . . .

Twice a week I run a support group called Beyond Alzheimer's for caregivers and family members of those with Alzheimer's and dementia. I look into haunted eyes that remind me of my own when my father was ill. I listen to stories of helplessness and loss and am continually moved by the bravery of those who wake up every morning not knowing who their loved one will be that day, or what will be lost. The only certainty with Alzheimer's is that more will be lost and the disease will always win in the end.[10]

Decide on Your Personal Brain-Care Action Plan

The good news is that your mental health responds to nurturing.

Make a list of things you can do to exercise your brain and post it on the refrigerator. For the activities that may take a little time, decide how much time a week you can spend on them. Be realistic and flexible. It's keeping up with the short-term goals that will get you to long-term success.

Here are a few basics that can help you get started:

- Make daily behavioral changes. Eat breakfast, read a short devotional message, choose three things you want to accomplish each day, include a social contact, get fresh air, and so on.
- Get regular medical checkups and comply with treatment plans. (Your physical health impacts your mental health.)
- Keep changing up your routines a little bit. It's good for your brain.
- Enlist others to help you stay on track (accountability buddies).
- Embrace health trends. Better nutrition and more physical and mental exercise will clear your head and invigorate you.
- Identify and reduce your bad habits. The damage may be reversible.

- Laugh more. Check out funny books and movies from the library.
- Go somewhere every day, and read everything you can get your hands on—food labels at the grocery store, church bulletins, or even junk mail.
- Make sure your daily lifestyle choices reflect your core values and goals.

Make Memories Part of Your Brain-Care Action Plan

It's a good idea to make a list of your special memories and add to it as often as you can. We know from personal experience that it's not always the big events that make a permanent impression on our minds. Sometimes it's the small, daily incidences that remain in our minds for a lifetime. If these are recorded, the fantasy and reality can be sorted out as memories grow old. Having journals with treasured memories will be a future blessing to you as well as a helpful aid to your caregivers.

Start gathering some of the following keepsakes and write down memories of the topics below. Adding more details in the coming years will be a blessing to you and your family.

- photo albums and scrapbooks
- notebook to jot down family memories such as:

milestones	vacations
holiday traditions	schools and churches
favorite friends	"firsts"
interesting facts about ancestors	happiness is . . .
	fears and mistakes
homes and cars	the little things
family jokes and sayings	hopes
honors, achievements	sports
pets	favorite foods
childhood	

What's Your Action Plan?

To make a difference in your long-term mental ability, you'll need to do more than just sporadically tweak a routine. You'll need a plan that will not only specifically list what you want to change but also determine when, where, and how you're going to do it. Committing to these behavioral changes will make a big difference. The best way to get something done is to begin.

Check what you will commit to now:

- [ ] fight procrastination ("I'll start after . . . ; it's not that important; I'm too busy right now.")

- [ ] read food labels at the grocery store—nutrition information and ingredients lists; look for three or more grams of whole-grain fiber, less than 5 percent sodium, and protein (*Red flag*: when first ingredients are sugar or aliases, refined grain, trans fats, or chemical additives)

- [ ] simplify your routines and prioritize your activities to decrease stress

- [ ] improve your sleep habits

- [ ] start eating more of the Mediterranean diet

- [ ] decrease caffeine and alcohol

- [ ] revive a special interest

- [ ] figure your body mass index (BMI)

- ☐ check your medications' product information for side effects
- ☐ try the 7 x 7 wake-up exercises
- ☐ consider vitamin and antioxidant needs
- ☐ schedule a health checkup with your doctor
- ☐ use your nondominant hand for everything you can
- ☐ don't go to bed hungry or after overeating
- ☐ vary your exercise routine
- ☐ exercise gently to moderately twenty to thirty minutes every day
- ☐ schedule social outings with family or friends
- ☐ eat more lean protein and less sugar
- ☐ read something every day (magazine, newspaper)
- ☐ avoid boredom
- ☐ review Memory Boosters exercises in this book
- ☐ eat "rainbow" foods—orange, red, blue, purple, and green
- ☐ learn how to do something new
- ☐ identify one thing that's stressful in your life and make a plan to address it

Try this plan for a week or two. If it isn't working for you after that stint, choose other options and make adjustments—but don't quit. At least you're off dead center and are doing something!

Conclusion

Have you ever noticed that every movie, book, sermon, or presentation gets summarized in one sentence for promotional purposes? The summary of this book might simply be, "Reduce your risk of mental decline." It's an action statement about making personal choices that can protect your memory and give you a better chance of making it through old age with your mind intact.

The insights and practical advice in this book are meant to be informative, supportive, and encouraging. I hope you will find them useful. Regardless of any poor choices you've made in the past, you can make better choices today. I've shared some of my personal stories, strengths, weaknesses, and most of all, my choices. Your choices matter too.

My hope is for each person to lead a healthy and happy life to the end. I want you to be gentle and patient with yourself and to relax in peace at the end of each day. As your life is enriched by God's love and grace, you, in turn, will be able to enrich the lives of those around you. Look at each day as an opportunity to make good choices for your spiritual, physical, emotional, and mental health.

God bless you on your personal journey.

Answer Key

What Do You Know?
    The statements are correct/true.

Warm-Up Vocabulary Quiz
    The correct answers are 1-C, 2-B, 3-A, 4-D, 5-A, 6-B, 7-C, 8-C, 9-C, 10-B.

Puzzle Power 1
    Interpretation: The man looking at the portrait has no brothers or sisters. His father's son is himself. So he is the father of the man in the portrait. The man is looking at a portrait of his son.

Historical Characters
    The characteristics are correct/true.

History of Ideas
    False. Several dates are out of order near the end.

Puzzle Power 2
    Interpretation: The one question to ask both men is, "What would he (the other man present) say?" The man who could not lie would say that the other man (who could not tell the truth)

would point in the wrong direction. The man who could not tell the truth would say that the other man (who could not lie) would point in the wrong direction also—not that the man who could not lie would lie, but rather the man who could not tell the truth would lie. Thus, the correct direction to go would be the opposite of what either man or both men said.

United States Government
    The statements are correct/true.

United States Constitution
    The amendments are correct/true.

Historical Ages
    The sequence is correct/true.

Historical Personalities
    The statements are correct/true.

Music and Memory
    The information is correct/true.

Conceptual Exercises
    The correct answer for each of them is "a."

Explorers' Passions and Purpose
    The facts are correct/true.

Literary Classics
    They are not all correct: Poe wrote "The Raven," not "The Crow."

Famous People in History
    The facts are correct/true.

Math Concepts
    The definitions are correct/true.

Biology Definitions
    The definitions are correct/true.

Pictures on Coins and Bills
    Number 9 is incorrect. It was proposed to change the picture on the fifty-dollar bill to Ronald Reagan, but it didn't happen. The correct answer is Ulysses S. Grant.

Functions of the Mind
    The statements are correct/true.

Know Your English
    False. The definitions for numbers 7 and 8 (adjective and adverb) are reversed.

Homographs
    1. ship/card = deck
    2. tree/car = trunk
    3. school/eye = pupil (exam and private are also possible)
    4. pillow/court = case
    5. river/money = bank (flow is possible)
    6. bed/paper = sheet
    7. army/water = tank
    8. tennis/noise = racket
    9. Egyptian/mother = mummy
    10. smoker/plumber = pipe

Bibliography

Abaya, Carol. "Is Your Life Being Squeezed?" The Sandwich Generation. http://www.sandwichgeneration.com/.

"Calculators: Life Expectancy." Social Security Administration. 2016. https://www.ssa.gov/planners/lifeexpectancy.html.

Cherry, Kendra. "7 Myths about the Brain." *Neuroscience and Biological Psychology*, January 8, 2016. https://www.verywell.com.

"Cognitive Assessment." Alzheimer's Association. 2016. http://www.alz.org/health-care-professionals/cognitive-tests-patient.

Congos, Dennis. "9 Types of Mnemonics for Better Memory." The Learning Center Exchange. http://www.learningassistance.com/2006/january/mnemonics.html.

"Diagnosis of Alzheimer's Disease and Dementia." Alzheimer's Association. http://www.alz.org/alzheimers_disease_diagnosis.asp.

Dillinger, Samantha. "The Most Important Goals." Ranker. 2016. http://www.ranker.com/list/most-important-life-goals-list/samantha-dillinger.

Helmuth, Laura. "Top Ten Myths about the Brain." *Science-Nature*. May 19, 2011. http://www.smithsonianmag.com/sciencenature/top-ten-myths-about-the-brain-178357288/.

LaFrance, Adrienne. "How Many Websites Are There?" *The Atlantic*, September 30, 2015. http://www.theatlantic.com /technology/archive/2015/09/how-many-websites-are -there/408151/.

Lee, Dick, and Delmar Hatesohl. "Listening: Our Most Used Communication Skill." The University of Missouri. 2015. http://extension.missouri.edu/p/CM150.

Mastin, Luke. "The Human Memory." 2010. http://www.human -memory.net/brain_neurons.html.

Matthews, Dale. "Staying Young." *Today's Better Life* (Summer 1992): 93–95.

Meynert, Barbara. "Growing Old Isn't for Sissies." Sage Vita. January 10, 2013. http://www.sagevita.com/learning /growing-old-isnt-for-sissies/.

Michelon, Pascale. "Brain Teaser to Exercise Your Cognitive Skills: Where Do Words Go?" SharpBrains. June 20, 2014. http://sharpbrains.com/blog/2014/06/20/brain-teaser-to -exercise-your-cognitive-skills-where-do-words-go/.

Minirth, Frank. *Boost Your Brainpower*. Grand Rapids: Revell, 2010.

———. *A Brilliant Mind: Proven Ways to Increase Your Brainpower*. Grand Rapids: Revell, 2007.

———. "Reach for the Blue Skies." *Today's Better Life* (Spring 1993): 39–41.

Minirth, Frank, and Paul Meier. *Happiness Is a Choice*. Grand Rapids: Baker Books, 1988.

Minirth, Frank, Paul Meier, Richard Flournoy, and Jane Mack. *Sweet Dreams*. Grand Rapids: Baker Books, 1985.

Raichle, Marcus E., and Debra A. Gusnard. "Appraising the Brain's Energy Budget." Proceedings of the National

Academy of Sciences 99, no. 16 (2002): 10237–39. http://
www.pnas.org/content/99/16/10237.full.

Reagan, Patti Davis. "An Open Letter to Will Ferrell." Books by
Patti Davis. April 28, 2016. http://booksbypattidavis.com
/an-open-letter-to-will-ferrell.

"Researchers DeBunk Myth of 'Right-Brain' and 'Left-Brain' Personality Traits." University of Utah Health Care. August 14,
2013. http://healthcare.utah.edu/publicaffairs/news/2013
/08/08-14-2013_brain_personality_traits.php.

Reuell, Peter. "Muting the Mozart Effect." *Harvard Gazette*,
December 11, 2013. www.news.harvard.edu/gazette/story
/2013/12/muting-the-mozart-effect/.

Sightings, Tom. *Sightings over Sixty* (blog). January 6, 2015.
http://sightingsat60.blogspot.com/.

Sperry, Roger W. "Split-Brain Approach to Learning Problems."
In Quarton, Melnechuk, and Schmitt, *The Neurosciences:
A Study Program*. New York: Rockefeller University Press,
1967, 714–22. people.uncw.edu/puente/sperry/sperry
papers/#1967.

"Symptoms and Causes." Mayo Foundation for Medical Education and Research. 2016. http://www.mayoclinic.org/dis
eases-conditions/alzheimers-disease/symptoms-causes/dxc
-20167103.

"The Ten Best Vocabulary Learning Tips." Sheppard Software.
2016. http://www.sheppardsoftware.com/vocabulary_tips
.htm.

"The World: Life Expectancy (2017)." geoba.se. http://www
.geoba.se/population.php?pc=world&type=15.

Vos Savant, Marilyn, and Leonore Fleischer. *Brain Building in
Just 12 Weeks*. New York: Bantam Books, 1990. http://
marilynvossavant.com.

Notes

Part 2 Memory Boosters

1. Vos Savant and Fleischer, *Brain Building*, 78.
2. Cherry, "7 Myths about the Brain."
3. Mastin, "The Human Memory."
4. Helmuth, "Top Ten Myths about the Brain."
5. Sperry, "Split-Brain Approach to Learning Problems."
6. "Researchers DeBunk Myth of 'Right-Brain' and 'Left-Brain' Personality Traits."
7. Reuell, "Muting the Mozart Effect."
8. Vos Savant and Fleischer, *Brain Building*, 94.
9. Sightings, *Sightings over Sixty* (blog).
10. Meynert, "Growing Old Isn't for Sissies."
11. Minirth, Meier, Flournoy, and Mack, *Sweet Dreams*, 45.
12. "Symptoms and Causes."
13. Matthews, "Staying Young," 95.
14. Congos, "9 Types of Mnemonics for Better Memory."
15. Adapted from Minirth, *A Brilliant Mind*, 129–30.
16. "The Ten Best Vocabulary Learning Tips."
17. Michelon, "Brain Teaser to Exercise Your Cognitive Skills."
18. Minirth, *Boost Your Brainpower*, 27.
19. "Cognitive Assessment."
20. "Diagnosis of Alzheimer's Disease and Dementia."

Part 3 Stress and Your Brain

1. Carol Abaya coined these terms. See Abaya, "Is Your Life Being Squeezed?" Social worker Dorothy Miller created the term "sandwich generation" in 1981. Journalist Abaya categorized the different scenarios involved in being a part of the

sandwich generation. She continues to study and expose what the term means as the trend grows.

Part 4 Anxiety and Your Brain

1. Lee and Hatesohl, "Listening."

Part 5 Memory and Purpose

1. Minirth, "Reach for the Blue Skies," 39.
2. Dillinger, "The Most Important Goals."
3. Minirth, "Reach for the Blue Skies," 39–40.
4. "Calculators: Life Expectancy."
5. "The World."
6. Minirth and Meier, *Happiness Is a Choice*, 174.
7. Raichle and Gusnard, "Appraising the Brain's Energy Budget."
8. Matthews, "Staying Young," 95.
9. LaFrance, "How Many Websites Are There?"
10. Reagan, "An Open Letter to Will Ferrell."

Frank Minirth, MD (1946–2015) was president of the Minirth Clinic in Richardson, Texas, and an adjunct professor at Dallas Theological Seminary. He was the author or coauthor of several books, including the bestselling *Happiness Is a Choice* and *Strong Memory, Sharp Mind*. For more information, visit www.minirth clinic.com.